Company's Coming®

4-Ingredient
Recipes

Jean Paré

www.companyscoming.com
visit our ↖website

Front Cover

1. Curry Noodle Bowl, page 48
2. Tangy Rice Parfaits, page 124
3. Spinach Cranberry Salad, page 39
4. Tuscan Pull-Aparts, page 26

Props courtesy of:
Canhome Global
Casa Bugatti
Totally Bamboo

Back Cover

1. Swirled Raisin Braid, page 25
2. Berry Bran Shake, page 56
3. Salmon-Sauced Bennies, page 49
4. Blueberry Cream Pancakes, page 50

Props courtesy of:
Danesco Inc.

Seventh Printing January 2011

Library and Archives Canada Cataloguing in Publication
Paré, Jean, date
4-ingredient recipes / Jean Paré.
(Original series)
Includes index.
ISBN 978-1-897069-00-4
1. Quick and easy cookery. I. Title. II. Title: Four-ingredient recipes.
III. Series: Paré, Jean, date-Original series.
TX833.5.P36 2006   641.5'55   C2005-907211-3

We gratefully acknowledge the following suppliers for their generous support of our Test and Photography Kitchens:

Broil King Barbecues
Corelle®
Hamilton Beach® Canada
Lagostina®
Proctor Silex® Canada
Tupperware®

Published by
Company's Coming Publishing Limited
2311 – 96 Street
Edmonton, Alberta, Canada T6N 1G3
Tel: 780-450-6223   Fax: 780-450-1857
www.companyscoming.com

Company's Coming is a registered trademark owned by Company's Coming Publishing Limited

We acknowledge the financial support of the Government of Canada through the Canada Book Fund for our publishing activities.

Printed in Canada

Get more great recipes...FREE!

click

search

print

cook

From apple pie to zucchini bread, we've got you covered. Browse our free online recipes for Guaranteed Great!™ results.

You can also sign up to receive our **FREE online newsletter**. You'll receive exclusive offers, FREE recipes & cooking tips, new title previews, and much more...all delivered to your in-box.

So don't delay, visit our website today!

www.companyscoming.com
visit our ↑ website

Company's Coming Cookbooks

Quick & easy recipes; everyday ingredients!

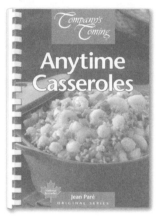

Original Series

- Softcover, 160 pages
- Lay-flat plastic comb binding
- Full-colour photos
- Nutrition information

Original Series

- Softcover, 160 pages
- Lay-flat plastic comb binding
- Full-colour photos
- Nutrition information

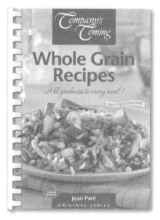

Original Series

- Softcover, 160 pages
- Lay-flat plastic comb binding
- Full-colour photos
- Nutrition information

2-in-1 Cookbook Collection

- Softcover, 256 pages
- Lay-flat plastic coil binding
- Full-colour photos
- Nutrition information

For a complete listing of our cookbooks, visit our website:
www.companyscoming.com

Table of Contents

Foreword

Appetizers

Breakfast

Lunch

Supper

Desserts & Snacks

Recipe Index

What's New!

The Company's Coming Story

Jean Paré (pronounced "jeen PAIR-ee") grew up understanding that the combination of family, friends and home cooking is the best recipe for a good life. From her mother, she learned to appreciate good cooking, while her father praised even her earliest attempts in the kitchen. When Jean left home, she took with her a love of cooking, many family recipes and an intriguing desire to read cookbooks as if they were novels!

"Never share a recipe you wouldn't use yourself."

When her four children had all reached school age, Jean volunteered to cater the 50th anniversary celebration of the Vermilion School of Agriculture, now Lakeland College, in Alberta, Canada. Working out of her home, Jean prepared a dinner for more than 1,000 people, launching a flourishing catering operation that continued for over 18 years. During that time, she had countless opportunities to test new ideas with immediate feedback—resulting in empty plates and contented customers! Whether preparing cocktail sandwiches for a house party or serving a hot meal for 1,500 people, Jean Paré earned a reputation for great food, courteous service and reasonable prices.

As requests for her recipes increased, Jean was often asked the question, "Why don't you write a cookbook?" Jean responded by teaming up with her son, Grant Lovig, in the fall of 1980 to form Company's Coming Publishing Limited. The publication of *150 Delicious Squares* on April 14, 1981 marked the debut of what would soon become one of the world's most popular cookbook series.

The company has grown since those early days when Jean worked from a spare bedroom in her home. Today, she continues to write recipes while working closely with the staff of the Recipe Factory, as the Company's Coming test kitchen is affectionately known.

There she fills the role of mentor, assisting with the development of recipes people most want to use for everyday cooking and easy entertaining. Every Company's Coming recipe is *kitchen-tested* before it is approved for publication.

Jean's daughter, Gail Lovig, is responsible for marketing and distribution, leading a team that includes sales personnel located in major cities across Canada. Company's Coming cookbooks are distributed in Canada, the United States, Australia and other world markets. Bestsellers many times over in English, Company's Coming cookbooks have also been published in French and Spanish.

Familiar and trusted in home kitchens around the world, Company's Coming cookbooks are offered in a variety of formats. Highly regarded as kitchen workbooks, the softcover Original Series, with its lay-flat plastic comb binding, is still a favourite among readers.

Jean Paré's approach to cooking has always called for *quick and easy recipes* using *everyday ingredients*. That view has served her well. The recipient of many awards, including the Queen Elizabeth Golden Jubilee Medal, Jean was appointed Member of the Order of Canada, her country's highest lifetime achievement honour.

Jean continues to gain new supporters by adhering to what she calls The Golden Rule of Cooking: *Never share a recipe you wouldn't use yourself.* It's an approach that has worked—*millions of times over!*

Foreword

Let's face it—after a full day of work, the last thing we want to face is a recipe listing 17 ingredients and directions more complicated than a computer manual. No wonder many of us have the phone number of our favourite takeout place memorized!

But what if all you had to do was toss together four ingredients to make a dish that will have your troops gathering eagerly around the table? *4-Ingredient Recipes* is full of easy ideas using convenient foods to prepare great-tasting meals. Our Lemon Tuna Fettuccine, for instance, calls for fettuccine noodles, garlic butter, a lemon and a can of tuna. Add a bowl of salad and you're done! It's so simple that even your kids can get dinner started.

And for tomorrow, try our Ginger Apricot Chicken. Marinate chicken breasts in Italian dressing, ginger and apricot jam in the morning, and you'll be all set for supper.

We've included tasty side dishes such as Salsa Rice, Sweet Onion Squash and Orange Basil Couscous. Get the gang into the kitchen, assign them each a dish and catch up on the day while you put a home-cooked meal on the table.

You'll also find breakfast and lunch ideas, along with mouth-watering desserts. Mudsicle Pie, anyone? How about Ooey Gooey Bars, Blondie Brownies or the divine Chocolate Crunch Cookies (featuring Skor bars as the secret component)? "Just four ingredients," you'll say airily, as you tick them off for your friends.

We've taken advantage of some of the interesting convenience products on your grocery shelves to save you cooking steps. Ingredients run from the everyday, such as peanut butter and cans of condensed soup, to the more exotic, like oyster sauce and chai tea concentrate. As usual, we've come up with delicious, kitchen-tested combinations that will make your four-ingredient dishes a hit with family and friends.

So file away that takeout phone number. With *4-Ingredient Recipes*, you'll be able to whip up simple, nourishing meals faster than your family can argue about pizza toppings. And you won't have to round up toonies for tipping!

Jean Paré

One, Two ... Free Four!

When our test kitchen sat down to plan *4-Ingredient Recipes*, we debated long and hard about what an ingredient was.

"How about water?" asked one. Well, water, though necessary in so many dishes (how do you cook pasta or rice without it?), wasn't really going to count, we decided.

"OK," said another, "but what about the salt we put into the water for pasta?"

"That just brings out the flavour of the pasta," declared a third. "It doesn't create a new flavour, the way basil or oregano would. You can hardly cook pasta without salt!"

After much discussion, we agreed that our "free" ingredients would be water, salt, pepper and the cooking oil needed for frying. All other ingredients had to stand up and be counted.

How We Tested These Recipes

- We use non-stick frying pans in our kitchens.
- A greased frying pan means 1 to 2 tsp. (5 to 10 mL) of cooking oil; well-greased means 1 tbsp. (15 mL) of oil or more.
- When we cook pasta in "boiling salted water," we recommend 1/2 tsp. (2 mL) salt per 4 cups (1 L) water.

- Unless we've indicated otherwise, we've used:
  - 1% milk
  - canola oil as cooking oil
  - the juice of fresh lemons and limes
  - the centre rack in the oven

Guaranteed Great™ Guidelines

For recipe success, follow these cooking tips:

- Read the recipe through.
- Gather and prepare (slice, chop, etc.) your ingredients.
- Use correct wet and dry measures. A liquid measuring cup has a rim to prevent liquids from spilling. A dry measure has no rim, allowing you to level off flour, etc., with a knife.

- To prevent packing the flour, spoon it into a dry measure.
- Don't substitute tub margarine for hard margarine when baking. Tub margarine contains water, which will affect the outcome.
- Use the correct size of saucepan, baking pan or casserole dish indicated in the recipe to avoid under or overcooking.

Salmon Cream Quiche

You'll be surprised how easy these elegant appetizers are to make,
and your guests will never know—unless they ask for the recipe!

Tub of smoked salmon spreadable cream cheese	8 oz.	250 g
Milk	1/2 cup	125 mL
Large eggs	2	2
Frozen mini tart shells, thawed	30	30

Process first 3 ingredients and a sprinkle of salt and pepper in blender or food processor until smooth.

Arrange tart shells on baking sheet. Pour cream cheese mixture into shells until almost full. Bake on bottom rack in 350°F (175°C) oven for about 30 minutes until filling is puffed and pastry is golden. Let stand on baking sheet for 10 minutes before removing from foil liners. Makes 30 mini quiche.

1 quiche: 73 Calories; 5.1 g Total Fat (2.1 g Mono, 0.5 g Poly, 2.1 g Sat); 20 mg Cholesterol;
5 g Carbohydrate; 0 g Fibre; 2 g Protein; 125 mg Sodium

Hawaiian Hammies

A good addition to a tropical theme buffet. Provide long cocktail
picks for this sweet and sour nibble so guests can help themselves.

Large green pepper, cut into 1 inch (2.5 cm) pieces	1	1
Ham sausage, cut into 1/4 inch (6 mm) slices	1 1/2 lbs.	680 g
Can of pineapple chunks, drained	14 oz.	398 mL
Sweet and sour sauce	1 1/2 cups	375 mL

Cook green pepper in large well-greased frying pan on medium for about 5 minutes, stirring occasionally, until tender-crisp.

Add remaining 3 ingredients. Stir. Cook for about 5 minutes, stirring occasionally, until heated through. Serves 12.

1 serving: 169 Calories; 7.7 g Total Fat (0.7 g Mono, 0.4 g Poly, 0.1 g Sat); 0 mg Cholesterol;
15 g Carbohydrate; 1 g Fibre; 10 g Protein; 641 mg Sodium

Spinach Cream Triangles

These flaky bundles can be made ahead and frozen. Brushing the pastry sheets with garlic butter instead of margarine will add extra good flavour.

Boxes of frozen chopped spinach (10 oz., 300 g, each), thawed and squeezed dry	2	2
Tub of vegetable light spreadable cream cheese	8 oz.	250 g
Frozen phyllo pastry sheets, thawed according to package directions	12	12
Hard margarine (or butter), melted	1/2 cup	125 mL

Combine spinach, cream cheese and a sprinkle of salt and pepper in medium bowl. Set aside.

Work with pastry sheets 1 at a time. Keep remaining sheets covered with damp tea towel to prevent drying. Place 1 sheet on work surface. Brush with margarine. Place second sheet on top, aligning edges. Brush with margarine. Layer with third pastry sheet. Brush with margarine. Cut lengthwise into 4 equal strips (see diagram 1). Spoon about 2 tbsp. (30 mL) spinach mixture onto end of 1 strip (see diagram 2). Fold pastry over filling to enclose, forming triangle (see diagram 3). Continue folding to end of strip (see diagrams 4, 5 and 6). Place on greased baking sheet. Cover with damp tea towel. Fill and fold remaining 3 strips. Repeat with remaining ingredients to make 16 triangles. Brush tops with remaining margarine. Bake in 350°F (175°C) oven for about 30 minutes until golden. Remove to wire rack to cool. Makes 16 triangles.

1 triangle: 139 Calories; 10 g Total Fat (5.1 g Mono, 1.2 g Poly, 3.1 g Sat); 10 mg Cholesterol; 9 g Carbohydrate; 1 g Fibre; 3 g Protein; 272 mg Sodium

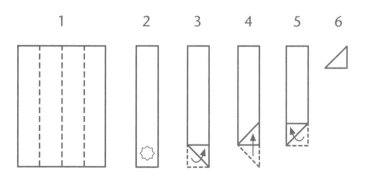

Thai Chicken Salad Wraps

*Rice paper rounds are easy to use. You'll have these assembled
in no time. Serve with extra peanut sauce for dipping.*

Lean ground chicken	1 lb.	454 g
Thai peanut sauce	3/4 cup	175 mL
Rice paper rounds (8 inch, 20 cm, diameter)	12	12
Bag of spring mix lettuce	5 oz.	142 g

Scramble-fry ground chicken in large greased frying pan on medium for about 10 minutes until no longer pink. Drain.

Add peanut sauce. Stir. Cool to room temperature.

Work with rice paper rounds 1 at a time. Soak 1 round in hot water in 9 x 9 inch (22 x 22 cm) pan for about 1 minute until softened. Place on work surface. Put about 1/2 cup (125 mL) lettuce on bottom half of round, leaving 1 inch (2.5 cm) edge. Spoon about 3 tbsp. (50 mL) chicken mixture on top of lettuce. Fold sides over filling. Roll up from bottom to enclose. Press seam against roll to seal. Place, seam-side down, on large serving platter. Cover with damp tea towel to prevent drying. Repeat with remaining ingredients to make 12 wraps. Cut wraps in half crosswise, for a total of 24 pieces.

1 piece: 82 Calories; 5.5 g Total Fat (1.3 g Mono, 0.7 g Poly, 0.8 g Sat); 0 mg Cholesterol; 4 g Carbohydrate; trace Fibre; 5 g Protein; 172 mg Sodium

Paré Pointer
Pigs are great sports fans. They're always rooting.

Taco Beef Snacks

Everyone will love these hand-held pastry pockets filled with
Tex-Mex flavours. Pack any leftovers in the kids' lunch bags the next day!

Lean ground beef	1 lb.	454 g
Grated medium Cheddar cheese	2 cups	500 mL
Envelope of reduced sodium taco seasoning mix	1 1/4 oz.	35 g
Tubes of refrigerator country-style biscuits (10 biscuits per tube), 12 oz. (340 g), each	3	3

Scramble-fry ground beef in large greased frying pan on medium for about 10 minutes until no longer pink. Drain.

Add cheese and taco seasoning. Stir well. Set aside.

Separate biscuits. Pat into 4 inch (10 cm) circles. Spoon beef mixture onto centre of circles. Fold circles in half over filling. Pinch edges to seal. Arrange on 2 greased baking sheets. Bake on separate racks in 350°F (175°C) oven for 15 to 20 minutes, switching position of baking sheets at halftime, until golden. Makes 30 taco snacks.

1 taco snack: 148 Calories; 5.8 g Total Fat (2.3 g Mono, 0.4 g Poly, 2.6 g Sat); 16 mg Cholesterol; 17 g Carbohydrate; trace Fibre; 7 g Protein; 561 mg Sodium

Paré Pointer

Does the transplant recipient of a gambler's heart now have a cheating heart?

Garlic Lime Pita Chips

Use commercial garlic butter that's flavoured
with wine or herbs for a special touch.

Medium lime	1	1
Garlic butter	1/4 cup	60 mL
Pita breads (3 inch, 7.5 cm, diameter), each split into 2 rounds	18	18
Grated Asiago cheese	1 cup	250 mL

Grate 1 tbsp. (15 mL) lime zest into small bowl. Set aside. Melt butter in small saucepan. Remove from heat. Squeeze and add 1 tbsp. (15 mL) lime juice. Stir.

Brush butter mixture on both sides of pita rounds. Cut each round into 4 wedges. Arrange, split-side up, on 2 ungreased baking sheets with sides.

Add cheese to zest in bowl. Stir. Sprinkle over pita wedges. Bake on separate racks in 350°F (175°C) oven for 12 to 15 minutes, switching position of baking sheets at halftime, until golden. Cool. Serves 12.

1 serving: 156 Calories; 6.9 g Total Fat (1.9 g Mono, 0.4 g Poly, 4.1 g Sat); 20 mg Cholesterol; 18 g Carbohydrate; 1 g Fibre; 5 g Protein; 254 mg Sodium

Pictured on page 17.

Black Olive Spread

This spread is rich and versatile! Serve with crackers, on sandwiches or even
toss with pasta. Use a good quality extra-virgin olive oil for best flavour.

Capers, rinsed and drained, divided	3 tbsp.	50 mL
Cans of pitted whole ripe olives (13 oz., 375 mL, each), drained	2	2
Garlic clove, minced (or 1/4 tsp., 1 mL, powder)	1	1
Olive oil	1/4 cup	60 mL

Reserve 1 tsp. (5 mL) capers for garnish. Put remaining capers into blender or food processor.

Add remaining 3 ingredients and a sprinkle of pepper. Process until smooth. Remove to small serving bowl. Garnish with reserved capers. Makes about 1 3/4 cups (425 mL).

2 tbsp. (30 mL): 56 Calories; 5.9 g Total Fat (4.3 g Mono, 0.5 g Poly, 0.8 g Sat); 0 mg Cholesterol; 1 g Carbohydrate; 1 g Fibre; 0 g Protein; 181 mg Sodium

Quesadilla Bites

There's quite a bite to the cheesy filling tucked inside
these warm wedges. Delicious, and easy to prepare!

Tub of vegetable light spreadable cream cheese	8 oz.	250 g
Flour tortillas (9 inch, 22 cm, diameter)	8	8
Grated havarti cheese	2 cups	500 mL
Cans of diced green chilies (4 oz., 113 g, each), drained	2	2

Spread cream cheese on tortillas, leaving 1/2 inch (12 mm) edge. Sprinkle havarti cheese and chilies on half of each tortilla. Fold tortillas in half over filling. Press down lightly. Spray both sides with cooking spray. Arrange on ungreased baking sheets. Bake in 400°F (205°C) oven for about 15 minutes, turning over after 10 minutes, until golden and cheese is melted. Cut each quesadilla into 6 wedges, for a total of 48 wedges.

1 wedge: 62 Calories; 3 g Total Fat (1 g Mono, 0.4 g Poly, 1.5 g Sat); 8 mg Cholesterol; 6 g Carbohydrate; trace Fibre; 3 g Protein; 176 mg Sodium

Spicy Feta Pâté

This creamy cheese pâté has a hint of sweetness and a jalapeño kick.
Good served with crackers or pita chips, or stuffed in celery sticks.

Block of cream cheese, softened	4 oz.	125 g
Crumbled feta cheese	1/2 cup	125 mL
Jellied cranberry sauce	2 tbsp.	30 mL
Jalapeño pepper, finely diced (see Tip, page 15)	1	1

Beat all 4 ingredients in medium bowl until well combined. Makes about 1 cup (250 mL).

2 tbsp. (30 mL): 107 Calories; 9 g Total Fat (2.3 g Mono, 0.3 g Poly, 5.9 g Sat); 32 mg Cholesterol; 3 g Carbohydrate; trace Fibre; 4 g Protein; 240 mg Sodium

Pictured on page 17.

Salmon-Stuffed Brie

A creamy salmon stuffing accented with lemon and dill is sandwiched between layers of Brie. A fancy, easy-to-make appetizer.

Medium lemon	1	1
Tub of smoked salmon spreadable cream cheese	8 oz.	250 g
Chopped fresh dill (or 1/2 tsp., 2 mL, dill weed)	2 tsp.	10 mL
Brie cheese rounds (4 oz., 125 g, each)	2	2

Grate 2 tsp. (10 mL) lemon zest into small bowl. Squeeze and add 2 tsp. (10 mL) lemon juice. Add cream cheese and dill. Beat until smooth.

Cut Brie cheese rounds in half horizontally (see Note). Spread cream cheese mixture on bottom halves. Replace tops. Makes 2 stuffed cheese rounds. Each cheese round cuts into 8 wedges, for a total of 16 wedges.

1 wedge: 88 Calories; 7.4 g Total Fat (2.2 g Mono, 0.2 g Poly, 4.5 g Sat); 25 mg Cholesterol; 1 g Carbohydrate; trace Fibre; 5 g Protein; 207 mg Sodium

Pictured on page 72.

Note: To easily halve a Brie cheese round, encircle the cheese along the centre of its circumference with a length of strong thread or plain dental floss. Crisscross the ends of the thread in front of you. Firmly pull both ends to slide the thread through the cheese.

 Hot peppers contain capsaicin in the seeds and ribs. Removing the seeds and ribs will reduce the heat. Wear rubber gloves when handling hot peppers and avoid touching your eyes. Wash your hands well afterwards.

Cajun Crackers

Kick it up a notch with these invitingly spicy, crisp crackers.
Perfect for dipping, or serve them with soup or salad.

Garlic butter, melted	2 tbsp.	30 mL
Flour tortillas (9 inch, 22 cm, diameter)	4	4
Grated Parmesan cheese	2 tbsp.	30 mL
Cajun seasoning	1 1/2 tsp.	7 mL

Brush butter on both sides of tortillas. Cut each tortilla into 8 wedges. Arrange on 2 ungreased baking sheets with sides.

Sprinkle with Parmesan cheese and seasoning. Bake on separate racks in 350°F (175°C) oven for about 14 minutes, switching position of baking sheets at halftime, until crisp and golden. Cool. Makes 32 crackers.

1 cracker: 33 Calories; 1.4 g Total Fat (0.5 g Mono, 0.2 g Poly, 0.6 g Sat); 2 mg Cholesterol; 4 g Carbohydrate; trace Fibre; 1 g Protein; 70 mg Sodium

1. Spicy Feta Pâté, page 14
2. Five-Spice Nut Crunch, page 129
3. Garlic Lime Pita Chips, page 13

Props courtesy of: Island Pottery Inc.

MMMussels

*A treat for seafood lovers. Thai broth subtly infuses
plump mussels with a wonderfully fragrant flavour.
A gingery mayonnaise provides the perfect accent.*

Thai-flavoured prepared chicken broth, divided	1 1/4 cups	300 mL
Fresh mussels, scrubbed and "beards" removed	4 lbs.	1.8 kg
Mayonnaise	1/2 cup	125 mL
Finely chopped pickled ginger slices	2 tbsp.	30 mL

Reserve 2 tbsp. (30 mL) broth in medium bowl. Put mussels into large
bowl. Lightly tap any that are opened. Discard any that do not close. Heat
remaining broth in large pot or Dutch oven on medium until boiling. Add
mussels. Cover. Cook for about 5 minutes, without stirring, until mussels
open. Remove mussels with slotted spoon to extra-large bowl. Discard any
unopened mussels.

Add mayonnaise and ginger to reserved broth. Stir. Serve with mussels.
Serves 10.

*1 serving: 232 Calories; 13.1 g Total Fat (6.1 g Mono, 4.1 g Poly, 1.6 g Sat); 52 mg Cholesterol;
7 g Carbohydrate; trace Fibre; 20 g Protein; 621 mg Sodium*

1. Orange Cranberry Wedges, page 28
2. Caramel Bubble Buns, page 23
3. Fast Focaccia, page 29

Props courtesy of: Island Pottery Inc.

Nutty Blue Cheese Dip

An all-purpose dip to serve with fresh vegetables. Or shape it into
a log, roll in finely chopped nuts, and chill to serve with crackers.

Block of cream cheese, softened	8 oz.	250 g
Salad dressing (or mayonnaise)	3 tbsp.	50 mL
Crumbled blue cheese	1/4 cup	60 mL
Chopped walnuts, toasted	2 tbsp.	30 mL
(see Tip, page 21)		

Beat cream cheese and salad dressing in medium bowl until smooth.

Add blue cheese and walnuts. Stir well. Makes about 1 1/3 cups (325 mL).

2 tbsp. (30 mL): 121 Calories; 11.7 g Total Fat (3.8 g Mono, 1.5 g Poly, 5.9 g Sat);
29 mg Cholesterol; 1 g Carbohydrate; trace Fibre; 3 g Protein; 146 mg Sodium

Crab Dip

Almonds and water chestnuts add a pleasant crunch
to this creamy dip. Serve with veggies or crackers.

Tub of creamy vegetable dip	10 1/2 oz.	296 mL
Can of sliced water chestnuts, drained	8 oz.	227 mL
and chopped		
Cans of crabmeat (4 1/4 oz., 120 g, each),	2	2
drained, cartilage removed, flaked		
Sliced blanched almonds, toasted	1/2 cup	125 mL
(see Tip, page 21)		

Combine first 3 ingredients in medium bowl. Transfer to serving bowl.

Sprinkle with almonds. Makes about 2 2/3 cups (650 mL).

2 tbsp. (30 mL): 46 Calories; 3.7 g Total Fat (1.5 g Mono, 0.4 g Poly, 1.6 g Sat); 5 mg Cholesterol;
2 g Carbohydrate; trace Fibre; 2 g Protein; 42 mg Sodium

Cheese Nippies

Rich cheese crackers topped with pecans. With a pleasant, spicy flavour,
they go nicely with green apple slices or grapes, and a glass of red wine.

Pastry for 2 crust 9 inch (22 cm) pie, your own or a mix		
Container of sharp cold pack Cheddar cheese	9 oz.	250 g
Cayenne pepper	1/2 tsp.	2 mL
Pecan halves, approximately	60	60

Mix first 3 ingredients with pastry blender in large bowl until mixture starts to come together. Turn out onto well-floured surface. Shape into slightly flattened disc. Roll out to 1/8 inch (3 mm) thickness. Cut out circles with 2 inch (5 cm) cookie cutter. Arrange about 2 inches (5 cm) apart on ungreased baking sheet.

Place 1 pecan half on each circle. Bake in 400°F (205°C) oven for 8 to 10 minutes until golden. Makes about 60 crackers.

1 cracker: 51 Calories; 4 g Total Fat (1.9 g Mono, 0.5 g Poly, 1.4 g Sat); 4 mg Cholesterol;
2 g Carbohydrate; trace Fibre; 1 g Protein; 53 mg Sodium

 To toast nuts, seeds or coconut, place them in an ungreased shallow frying pan. Heat on medium for 3 to 5 minutes, stirring often, until golden. To bake, spread them evenly in an ungreased shallow pan. Bake in a 350°F (175°C) oven for 5 to 10 minutes, stirring or shaking often, until golden.

Feta Crescent Swirls

Sweet, buttery pastries filled with zesty cheese.
Serve these with a bowl of soup for a light lunch or supper.

Crumbled feta cheese	1/4 cup	60 mL
Garlic butter	2 tbsp.	30 mL
Sweet chili sauce	2 tbsp.	30 mL
Tubes of refrigerator crescent-style rolls (8 rolls per tube), 8 1/2 oz. (235 g), each	2	2

Combine first 3 ingredients in small bowl. Set aside.

Unroll 1 tube of dough on lightly floured surface. Press perforations together to form 8 x 13 inch (20 x 33 cm) rectangle. Spread cheese mixture on dough, leaving 1/2 inch (12 mm) edge. Unroll second tube of dough on top of cheese mixture, aligning edges with bottom layer. Lightly press perforations together. Lightly press top layer. Pinch dough along edges to seal. Cut crosswise into 12 equal strips (see diagram 1). Twist 1 strip several times. It will lengthen to about 12 inches (30 cm). Loosely coil on baking sheet, tucking end under (see diagram 2). Repeat with remaining strips to make 12 swirls. Bake in 375°F (190°C) oven for 15 to 20 minutes until golden. Makes 12 swirls.

1 swirl: 99 Calories; 6.6 g Total Fat (1.2 g Mono, 0.3 g Poly, 1.7 g Sat); 8 mg Cholesterol; 8 g Carbohydrate; trace Fibre; 2 g Protein; 282 mg Sodium

Pictured on page 89.

1

2

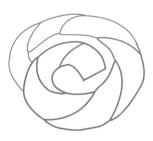

Caramel Bubble Buns

Sweet caramel glazes a ring of soft, gooey pull-aparts.
You won't believe how simple it is to create this
sweet treat for brunch or coffee break. A real winner!

Packages of frozen unbaked dinner rolls (1 lb., 454 g, each)	2	2
Hard margarine (or butter)	1/2 cup	125 mL
Brown sugar, packed	1/2 cup	125 mL
Box of butterscotch pudding powder (not instant), 6 serving size	1	1

Thaw covered dough at room temperature for 1 1/2 hours.

Heat and stir margarine and brown sugar in small saucepan on medium for about 6 minutes until boiling. Remove from heat.

Grease 12 cup (3 L) bundt pan. Cut dinner rolls in half. Roll into balls. Arrange 1/2 of balls in pan. Sprinkle with 1/2 of pudding powder. Drizzle with 1/2 of margarine mixture. Arrange remaining balls on top. Sprinkle with remaining pudding powder. Drizzle with remaining margarine mixture. Cover loosely with greased waxed paper and tea towel. Let stand in oven with light on and door closed for about 1 1/2 hours until doubled in size. Bake in 350°F (175°C) oven for about 30 minutes until golden. Let stand in pan on wire rack for 5 minutes before inverting onto large serving plate. Makes about 48 buns.

1 bun: 96 Calories; 3.5 g Total Fat (2 g Mono, 0.4 g Poly, 0.8 g Sat); 0 mg Cholesterol; 15 g Carbohydrate; 1 g Fibre; 2 g Protein; 174 mg Sodium

Pictured on page 18.

Onion Flatbread

This quick bread, with a distinct onion flavour and a
poppy seed topping, is great served with soup or stew.

Biscuit mix	2 cups	500 mL
Onion flakes	1 tbsp.	15 mL
Hard margarine (or butter), melted	1 tbsp.	15 mL
Poppy seeds	1/2 tsp.	2 mL

Combine biscuit mix and onion flakes in medium bowl. Make a well in centre. Add 1/2 cup (125 mL) water to well. Stir until soft dough forms. Turn out onto greased baking sheet. Pat out dough to 9 inch (22 cm) circle.

Brush with margarine. Sprinkle with poppy seeds. Bake in 450°F (230°C) oven for about 10 minutes until golden. Cuts into 12 wedges.

1 wedge: 114 Calories; 5.3 g Total Fat (2.3 g Mono, 1.7 g Poly, 1 g Sat); 0 mg Cholesterol;
15 g Carbohydrate; trace Fibre; 2 g Protein; 299 mg Sodium

Variation: Instead of poppy seeds, use ground walnuts or finely chopped fresh rosemary.

Tomato-Topped Biscuits

Cheesy, herb-crusted biscuits topped with fresh tomato. A delight to serve!

Tube of refrigerator country-style biscuits (10 biscuits per tube)	12 oz.	340 g
Basil pesto	1/3 cup	75 mL
Grated mozzarella cheese	1 1/4 cups	300 mL
Large tomatoes, each cut into 5 slices	2	2

Separate biscuits. Pat into 3 1/2 inch (9 cm) circles. Arrange about 2 inches (5 cm) apart on greased baking sheet with sides.

Spread pesto on circles. Sprinkle with cheese. Bake in 375°F (190°C) oven for about 12 minutes until golden and cheese is bubbling.

Top with tomato slices. Sprinkle with pepper. Makes 10 biscuits.

1 biscuit: 163 Calories; 7.8 g Total Fat (3.8 g Mono, 0.8 g Poly, 2.8 g Sat); 12 mg Cholesterol;
18 g Carbohydrate; trace Fibre; 6 g Protein; 485 mg Sodium

Swirled Raisin Braid

*This attractive raisin braid is perfect for breakfast
or brunch. Delicious toasted too.*

Frozen white bread dough, covered and thawed in refrigerator overnight	1	1
Dark raisins	1/4 cup	60 mL
Cocoa, sifted if lumpy	2 tbsp.	30 mL
Fancy (mild) molasses	1 tbsp.	15 mL

Cut dough into 3 equal portions. Set 1 portion aside.

Combine remaining 3 ingredients and 1 tsp. (5 mL) water in medium bowl. Add 2 dough portions. Knead in bowl for about 3 minutes until dough is marbled with cocoa mixture. Divide in half. Roll into 12 inch (30 cm) long ropes with slightly tapered ends. Roll plain dough portion into 12 inch (30 cm) long rope. Lay ropes side by side, with plain rope in the middle, on work surface. Pinch ropes together at one end. Braid ropes. Pinch together at opposite end. Tuck ends under. Place on greased baking sheet. Cover with greased waxed paper and tea towel. Let stand in oven with light on and door closed for about 1 hour until almost doubled in size. Bake in 350°F (175°C) oven for about 25 minutes until golden and hollow sounding when tapped. Remove to wire rack to cool. Cuts into 20 slices.

1 slice: 70 Calories; 0.9 g Total Fat (0.4 g Mono, 0.2 g Poly, 0.2 g Sat); 0 mg Cholesterol; 14 g Carbohydrate; 1 g Fibre; 2 g Protein; 123 mg Sodium

Pictured on page 53 and on back cover.

Rugelach Roll-Ups

A traditional Hanukkah treat, Rugelach are crescent-shaped cookies filled with fruit and nuts or with jam. Delicious any time, we've filled our version with a tasty combination of raspberry jam and ginger. Yum!

Tube of refrigerator crescent-style rolls (8 rolls per tube)	8 1/2 oz.	235 g
Raspberry jam	1/4 cup	60 mL
Minced crystallized ginger	1 tbsp.	15 mL
Ground almonds	8 tsp.	40 mL

Unroll dough. Separate into triangles.

Combine jam and ginger in small bowl. Spread on triangles, leaving 1/4 inch (6 mm) edge at wide end.

Sprinkle with almonds. Roll up triangles from wide end toward point. Place rolls, point-side down, on greased baking sheet. Bake in 375°F (190°C) oven for 10 to 12 minutes until golden. Makes 8 roll-ups.

1 roll-up: 86 Calories; 3.1 g Total Fat (0.5 g Mono, 0.2 g Poly, 0.1 g Sat); 0 mg Cholesterol; 14 g Carbohydrate; trace Fibre; 1 g Protein; 147 mg Sodium

Pictured on page 54.

Tuscan Pull-Aparts

Soft and savoury, with the rich flavours of ripe olives and Parmesan cheese. Use commercial garlic butter that has added wine or herbs to make these buns extra tasty.

Frozen white bread dough, covered and thawed in refrigerator overnight	1	1
Garlic butter	1/4 cup	60 mL
Grated Parmesan cheese	1/2 cup	125 mL
Can of sliced ripe olives, chopped	4 1/2 oz.	125 mL

(continued on next page)

Breads

Cut dough into 12 equal portions. Roll into balls.

Melt butter in small saucepan. Remove from heat. Measure Parmesan cheese into small shallow dish. Dip balls in butter and roll in Parmesan cheese until coated. Arrange 8 balls in greased 9 x 5 x 3 inch (22 x 12.5 x 7.5 cm) loaf pan.

Sprinkle with olives. Place remaining 4 balls along centre of first layer. Drizzle with remaining butter. Sprinkle with remaining Parmesan cheese. Cover with greased waxed paper and tea towel. Let stand in oven with light on and door closed for about 40 minutes until doubled in size. Bake in 350°F (175°C) oven for 25 minutes. Cover loosely with foil. Bake for another 10 minutes. Let stand in pan for 10 minutes before removing to wire rack to cool. Makes 12 pull-aparts.

1 pull-apart: 161 Calories; 7.2 g Total Fat (2.5 g Mono, 0.5 g Poly, 3.7 g Sat); 15 mg Cholesterol; 19 g Carbohydrate; 1 g Fibre; 5 g Protein; 359 mg Sodium

Pictured on front cover.

Garlic Cheese Loaf

This restaurant-style garlic cheese bread speckled with ripe olives has an irresistible flavour! Great served with a main course salad.

Garlic butter, softened	1/3 cup	75 mL
French bread loaf, halved horizontally	1	1
Grated Mexican cheese blend	2 cups	500 mL
Can of sliced ripe olives, chopped	4 1/2 oz.	125 mL

Spread butter on both halves of loaf. Place, buttered-side up, on ungreased baking sheet.

Sprinkle with cheese and olives. Bake in 400°F (205°C) oven for about 15 minutes until cheese is melted and bread is heated through. Cut each half into 16 pieces, for a total of 32 pieces.

1 piece: 88 Calories; 5.1 g Total Fat (1.6 g Mono, 0.3 g Poly, 2.9 g Sat); 13 mg Cholesterol; 8 g Carbohydrate; trace Fibre; 3 g Protein; 165 mg Sodium

Pesto Parmesan Biscuits

Perfect with soup or stew, or serve on the side with an omelet for brunch.

Biscuit mix	2 cups	500 mL
Grated Parmesan cheese	2 tbsp.	30 mL
Milk, divided	2/3 cup	150 mL
Sun-dried tomato pesto	1 tbsp.	15 mL

Combine biscuit mix and Parmesan cheese in medium bowl. Make a well in centre.

Reserve 2 tbsp. (30 mL) milk in small cup. Combine remaining milk and pesto in small bowl. Add to well. Stir until just moistened. Turn out dough onto lightly floured surface. Knead 8 to 10 times. Roll out to 1/2 inch (12 mm) thickness. Cut out circles with lightly floured 2 inch (5 cm) biscuit cutter. Arrange about 1/2 inch (12 mm) apart on greased baking sheet. Brush with reserved milk. Bake in 450°F (230°C) oven for about 10 minutes until firm and golden. Makes about 12 biscuits.

1 biscuit: 115 Calories; 4.8 g Total Fat (1.9 g Mono, 1.6 g Poly, 1.1 g Sat); 1 mg Cholesterol; 15 g Carbohydrate; 0 g Fibre; 3 g Protein; 316 mg Sodium

Pictured on page 36.

Orange Cranberry Wedges

Cranberry-studded, scone-like wedges have a delicate orange flavour.

Large orange	1	1
Biscuit mix	2 cups	500 mL
Orange-flavoured dried cranberries	1 cup	250 mL
Vanilla-flavoured milk	1/3 cup	75 mL

Grate 1 tbsp. (15 mL) orange zest into medium bowl. Add biscuit mix and cranberries. Stir. Make a well in centre.

Squeeze and measure 1/3 cup (75 mL) orange juice into small bowl. Add milk. Stir. Add to well. Stir until just moistened. Spread in greased 8 inch (20 cm) round pan. Bake in 350°F (175°C) oven for about 30 minutes until wooden pick inserted in centre comes out clean. Let stand in pan for 10 minutes before inverting onto wire rack. Cuts into 12 wedges.

1 wedge: 122 Calories; 3.6 g Total Fat (1.3 g Mono, 1.3 g Poly, 0.7 g Sat); 0 mg Cholesterol; 20 g Carbohydrate; 2 g Fibre; 2 g Protein; 292 mg Sodium

Pictured on page 18.

Fast Focaccia

It's a snap to make focaccia bread using biscuit mix.
Garlic-flavoured olive oil infuses the bread with Italian flavours.
Serve with your favourite pasta dish.

Italian seasoning, divided	3 tsp.	15 mL
Biscuit mix	3 cups	750 mL
Milk	1 cup	250 mL
Garlic-flavoured olive oil, divided	3 tbsp.	50 mL

Reserve 1 tsp. (5 mL) seasoning in small cup. Put remaining seasoning into large bowl. Add biscuit mix. Stir. Make a well in centre.

Add milk to well. Stir until just moistened.

Brush 9 × 9 inch (22 × 22 cm) pan with 1 tbsp. (15 mL) olive oil. Press dough into pan. Poke indentations on surface of dough with fingers. Drizzle remaining olive oil over dough. Sprinkle with reserved seasoning. Bake in 400°F (205°C) oven for about 25 minutes until golden, and wooden pick inserted in centre comes out clean. Let stand in pan for 15 minutes. Cut into 4 squares. Cut squares in half diagonally, for a total of 8 triangles.

1 triangle: 281 Calories; 13.3 g Total Fat (6.6 g Mono, 3.4 g Poly, 2.5 g Sat); 1 mg Cholesterol; 35 g Carbohydrate; trace Fibre; 5 g Protein; 857 mg Sodium

Pictured on page 18.

Paré Pointer
What do prisoners use to talk with each other? Cell phones.

Lemon Poppy Seed Biscuits

A quick solution when you're craving something sweet.
These gooey biscuits are sure to satisfy!

Lemon curd (not spread)	2/3 cup	150 mL
Chopped walnuts (or pecans)	2 tbsp.	30 mL
Poppy seeds	1 tbsp.	15 mL
Tube of refrigerator country-style biscuits (10 biscuits per tube)	12 oz.	340 g

Spoon lemon curd into 10 greased muffin cups. Sprinkle with walnuts and poppy seeds.

Separate biscuits. Place in prepared muffin cups. Bake in 425°F (220°C) oven for 12 to 15 minutes until golden. Immediately invert onto wire rack set on baking sheet. Makes 10 biscuits.

1 biscuit: 179 Calories; 6.9 g Total Fat (2.8 g Mono, 1.9 g Poly, 1.6 g Sat); 26 mg Cholesterol; 27 g Carbohydrate; trace Fibre; 4 g Protein; 603 mg Sodium

Parmesan Olive Biscuits

Chopped olives in cheesy biscuits create a nice match for soup or salad.
Kalamata olives in place of ripe olives will produce a bolder, saltier taste.

Biscuit mix	2 cups	500 mL
Grated Parmesan cheese	2/3 cup	150 mL
Can of sliced ripe olives, chopped	4 1/2 oz.	125 mL
Milk	2/3 cup	150 mL

Combine first 3 ingredients in medium bowl. Make a well in centre.

Add milk to well. Stir until just moistened. Drop, using 2 tbsp. (30 mL) for each biscuit, about 2 inches (5 cm) apart onto greased baking sheet. Bake in 450°F (230°C) oven for about 12 minutes until golden. Makes about 15 biscuits.

1 biscuit: 112 Calories; 5.2 g Total Fat (2 g Mono, 1.3 g Poly, 1.6 g Sat); 4 mg Cholesterol; 12 g Carbohydrate; trace Fibre; 4 g Protein; 349 mg Sodium

Pictured on page 108.

Creamy Potato Salad

Smoky bits of bacon and a peppery, creamy dressing coat
chunks of potato and dill pickle in this flavourful salad. Tastes
even better made the day before and chilled overnight.

Red baby potatoes	1 lb.	454 g
Bacon slices, cooked crisp and crumbled	6	6
Peppercorn ranch dressing	1/3 cup	75 mL
Chopped dill pickle (or tangy dill relish)	2 tbsp.	30 mL

Cook potatoes in boiling salted water in medium saucepan until just tender. Drain. Transfer to medium bowl. Chill, uncovered, for about 2 hours until cold. Cut potatoes into quarters. Return to same bowl.

Add remaining 3 ingredients. Toss gently. Cover. Chill for at least 1 hour to blend flavours. Makes about 2 1/2 cups (625 mL). Serves 4.

1 serving: 226 Calories; 12.5 g Total Fat (6.5 g Mono, 3.2 g Poly, 2.2 g Sat); 14 mg Cholesterol; 23 g Carbohydrate; 2 g Fibre; 6 g Protein; 351 mg Sodium

Blue Cheese Pear Salad

Toasted pecans complement the bold flavour of blue cheese in this lovely salad.
Juicy pears make this delicious as is, or toss with a sweet vinaigrette.

Mixed salad greens, lightly packed	5 cups	1.25 L
Fresh pears, sliced	2	2
Pecan pieces, toasted (see Tip, page 21)	1/3 cup	75 mL
Crumbled blue cheese	1/3 cup	75 mL

Put all 4 ingredients into large bowl. Toss gently. Makes about 6 1/2 cups (1.6 L). Serves 4.

1 serving: 172 Calories; 10.9 g Total Fat (5.3 g Mono, 2 g Poly, 2.8 g Sat); 9 mg Cholesterol; 17 g Carbohydrate; 4 g Fibre; 5 g Protein; 182 mg Sodium

Pictured on page 35.

Tomato Bocconcini Salad

Eye-catching! Serve this classic salad with fresh, crusty baguette slices to dip into the dressing.

Roma (plum) tomatoes, cut into 1/4 inch (6 mm) slices	1 lb.	454 g
Container of bocconcini cheese, cut into 1/4 inch (6 mm) slices	7 oz.	200 g
Chopped fresh basil	1/3 cup	75 mL
Balsamic vinaigrette	1/4 cup	60 mL

Arrange tomato and cheese slices alternately in circular pattern around edge and in centre of large serving platter. Sprinkle generously with salt and freshly ground pepper.

Sprinkle with basil. Drizzle with vinaigrette. Serves 4.

1 serving: 174 Calories; 11.6 g Total Fat (3.5 g Mono, 0.6 g Poly, 6.9 g Sat); 41 mg Cholesterol; 8 g Carbohydrate; 1 g Fibre; 11 g Protein; 205 mg Sodium

Pictured on page 107.

Orange Fennel Salad

A delectable, refreshing salad that's easy to make.

Fennel bulb (white part only), quartered lengthwise and thinly sliced	1	1
Medium oranges, peeled and segmented (see Tip, page 33)	6	6
Maple (or maple-flavoured) syrup	1/4 cup	60 mL
Dijon mustard	1 tbsp.	15 mL

Put fennel and orange segments into large bowl. Toss gently.

Combine syrup and mustard in small cup. Drizzle over salad. Toss gently. Makes about 5 1/2 cups (1.4 L). Serves 6.

1 serving: 113 Calories; 0.4 g Total Fat (0.1 g Mono, 0.1 g Poly, 0.1 g Sat); 0 mg Cholesterol; 28 g Carbohydrate; 2 g Fibre; 2 g Protein; 56 mg Sodium

Curried Broccoli Slaw

Toasting the curry powder gives it a mellow flavour.
A great side for poached fish or roasted chicken.

Curry powder	1 tsp.	5 mL
Ranch dressing	1/2 cup	125 mL
Bag of broccoli slaw	12 oz.	340 g
Pecan pieces, toasted (see Tip, page 21)	1/2 cup	125 mL

Heat and stir curry powder in small frying pan on medium-low for about 5 minutes until fragrant. Transfer to small bowl. Cool.

Add dressing. Stir well.

Put broccoli slaw into large bowl. Add curry mixture. Stir until coated. Chill for at least 1 hour to blend flavours.

Sprinkle with pecan pieces just before serving. Makes about 3 1/2 cups (875 mL). Serves 4.

1 serving: 261 Calories; 22 g Total Fat (13 g Mono, 6.6 g Poly, 1.7 g Sat); 9 mg Cholesterol; 13 g Carbohydrate; 4 g Fibre; 4 g Protein; 254 mg Sodium

 To segment an orange, trim a small slice of peel from both ends so the flesh is exposed. Place the orange, bottom cut-side down, on a cutting board. Remove the peel with a sharp knife, cutting down and around the flesh, leaving as little pith as possible. Over a small bowl, cut on either side of the membranes to release the segments.

Wild Rice Salad

Chilling this salad will bring out the earthy flavours.
Perfect for a picnic or patio lunch.

Package of long grain and wild rice mix (with seasoning packet)	6 1/4 oz.	180 g
Chopped dried cherries	1/2 cup	125 mL
Slivered almonds, toasted (see Tip, page 21)	1/2 cup	125 mL
Blue cheese dressing	1/3 cup	75 mL

Combine rice with seasoning packet and 2 1/2 cups (625 mL) water in medium saucepan. Bring to a boil. Reduce heat to medium-low. Simmer, covered, for about 30 minutes until liquid is absorbed. Remove from heat. Let stand, covered, for 5 minutes. Transfer to large bowl. Cool to room temperature.

Add cherries, almonds and a sprinkle of salt and pepper. Stir. Drizzle with dressing. Stir well. Makes about 4 cups (1 L). Serves 4.

1 serving: 420 Calories; 20.9 g Total Fat (12.1 g Mono, 5.9 g Poly, 1.9 g Sat); 4 mg Cholesterol; 52 g Carbohydrate; 3 g Fibre; 9 g Protein; 722 mg Sodium

1. Lemon Coconut Angel, page 121
2. Polynesian Chicken, page 97
3. Blue Cheese Pear Salad, page 31

Props courtesy of: Casa Bugatti

Salads & Dressings

Antipasto Pasta Salad

Tangy-sweet antipasto flavour coats spiral pasta.
A tasty side salad to serve with baked or grilled herbed chicken.

Rotini (or other spiral) pasta	3 cups	750 mL
Jar of antipasto	9 oz.	250 g
Jar of marinated artichoke hearts, drained and larger pieces cut in half	6 oz.	170 mL
Coarsely crumbled feta cheese	1/2 cup	125 mL

Cook pasta in boiling salted water in large uncovered pot or Dutch oven for 8 to 10 minutes until tender but firm. Drain. Rinse with cold water. Drain well. Put into large bowl.

Add remaining 3 ingredients. Toss gently. Makes about 7 cups (1.75 L). Serves 6.

1 serving: 251 Calories; 3.6 g Total Fat (0.7 g Mono, 0.4 g Poly, 2.2 g Sat); 12 mg Cholesterol; 41 g Carbohydrate; 3 g Fibre; 10 g Protein; 436 mg Sodium

1. Pesto Parmesan Biscuits, page 28
2. Garlic Chicken Pasta, page 92
3. Curry Vegetable Soup, page 45

Props courtesy of: Casa Bugatti

Asian Cucumber Salad

Rice vinegar lends a piquant tang to sweet, dressed cucumbers.
Double the chili paste for added zip.

Rice vinegar	1/4 cup	60 mL
Hoisin sauce	2 tbsp.	30 mL
Chili paste (sambal oelek)	1/2 tsp.	2 mL
Unpeeled English cucumbers, halved lengthwise and cut diagonally into 1/4 inch (6 mm) slices	2	2

Combine first 3 ingredients in large bowl.

Add cucumber. Stir until coated. Chill for 2 to 3 hours, stirring once or twice, to blend flavours. Makes about 4 cups (1 L). Serves 6.

1 serving: 31 Calories; 0.2 g Total Fat (0 g Mono, 0.1 g Poly, 0.1 g Sat); 0 mg Cholesterol; 7 g Carbohydrate; 1 g Fibre; 1 g Protein; 137 mg Sodium

Savoury Apple Slaw

A savoury twist on coleslaw. Serve this with grilled cheese sandwiches,
or try it with a little Cheddar cheese as a wrap filling.

Dijon-flavoured mayonnaise	1/2 cup	125 mL
Tart medium cooking apples (such as Granny Smith), peeled and julienned (see Note)	2	2
Broccoli slaw	2 cups	500 mL
Julienned honey ham	2 cups	500 mL

Put mayonnaise into large bowl. Add apple. Stir gently until coated.

Add broccoli slaw, ham and a sprinkle of salt and pepper. Stir gently. Makes about 5 cups (1.25 L). Serves 6.

1 serving: 240 Calories; 18.3 g Total Fat (9.8 g Mono, 5.5 g Poly, 2.3 g Sat); 35 mg Cholesterol; 9 g Carbohydrate; 2 g Fibre; 11 g Protein; 823 mg Sodium

Note: To julienne, cut into very thin strips that resemble matchsticks.

Spinach Cranberry Salad

This salad can be on the table in no time! Toasted nuts
and dried berries add a delicious boost to greens and juicy oranges.
The brilliant colours say "healthy and fresh."

Bag of fresh spinach	6 oz.	170 g
Pecan halves, toasted (see Tip, page 21)	1/2 cup	125 mL
Orange-flavoured dried cranberries	1/4 cup	60 mL
Medium oranges	3	3

Put first 3 ingredients into large bowl. Toss.

Squeeze juice from 1 orange. Set aside. Peel remaining 2 oranges. Cut oranges crosswise into 1/4 inch (6 mm) slices. Cut slices in half. Add to spinach mixture. Drizzle with juice. Sprinkle with salt and pepper. Toss gently. Makes about 6 1/2 cups (1.6 L). Serves 4.

1 serving: 165 Calories; 10 g Total Fat (6 g Mono, 2.5 g Poly, 0.8 g Sat); 0 mg Cholesterol; 19 g Carbohydrate; 5 g Fibre; 3 g Protein; 34 mg Sodium

Pictured on front cover.

Bruschetta Lentil Salad

Olives, lentils and feta cheese make an appetizing and hearty salad.
Serve with crusty bread to soak up the juices.

Can of lentils, rinsed and drained	19 oz.	540 mL
Bruschetta topping	1 1/2 cups	375 mL
Cubed feta cheese	1 cup	250 mL
Can of sliced ripe olives, drained	4 1/2 oz.	125 mL

Put all 4 ingredients into large bowl. Mix well. Makes about 4 1/2 cups (1.1 L). Serves 6.

1 serving: 150 Calories; 6.9 g Total Fat (1.9 g Mono, 0.4 g Poly, 4.2 g Sat); 24 mg Cholesterol; 15 g Carbohydrate; 4 g Fibre; 9 g Protein; 659 mg Sodium

Feta Beet Salad

Sweet bites of beet and salty feta cheese create an interesting salad you're sure to enjoy.

Bag of mixed salad greens	5 oz.	142 g
Chopped pickled beets (3 tbsp., 50 mL, juice reserved)	1 cup	250 mL
Crumbled feta cheese	1 cup	250 mL
Spicy olive oil with herbs	2 tbsp.	30 mL

Put first 3 ingredients into large bowl. Toss gently.

Combine reserved beet juice and olive oil in small cup. Drizzle over salad. Toss gently. Makes about 6 cups (1.5 L). Serves 4.

1 serving: 173 Calories; 11.1 g Total Fat (3.6 g Mono, 0.5 g Poly, 6.5 g Sat); 36 mg Cholesterol; 12 g Carbohydrate; 2 g Fibre; 7 g Protein; 623 mg Sodium

Couscous Date Salad

Tangy raspberry vinaigrette offsets sweet dates in this delicious pilaf-like salad. Good with grilled chicken or kabobs.

Package of couscous with fruit and nuts	7 oz.	198 g
Chopped unpeeled English cucumber	2 cups	500 mL
Chopped pitted dates	1/2 cup	125 mL
Raspberry vinaigrette	1/4 cup	60 mL

Bring 1 1/2 cups (375 mL) water to a boil in medium saucepan. Add couscous. Stir. Return to a boil. Remove from heat. Let stand, covered, for 5 minutes. Fluff with a fork. Transfer to large bowl. Chill, uncovered, for 30 minutes.

Add cucumber and dates. Toss. Drizzle with vinaigrette. Toss well. Makes about 5 cups (1.25 L). Serves 6.

1 serving: 182 Calories; 2.1 g Total Fat (1.2 g Mono, 0.3 g Poly, 0.3 g Sat); 0 mg Cholesterol; 38 g Carbohydrate; 3 g Fibre; 4 g Protein; 330 mg Sodium

Pepper Berry Vinaigrette

Match this vinaigrette with a spinach or beet salad,
or drizzle over Blue Cheese Pear Salad, page 31.

Olive (or cooking) oil	1/3 cup	75 mL
Mixed berry jam	1/4 cup	60 mL
Balsamic vinegar	1/4 cup	60 mL
Pepper	1/2 tsp.	2 mL

Process all 4 ingredients in blender or food processor until smooth. Store in airtight container in refrigerator for up to 1 week. Makes about 3/4 cup (175 mL).

2 tbsp. (30 mL): 142 Calories; 12.1 g Total Fat (8.9 g Mono, 1 g Poly, 1.6 g Sat); 0 mg Cholesterol; 9 g Carbohydrate; trace Fibre; 0 g Protein; 6 mg Sodium

Cranberry Vinaigrette

This is a great way to use up that little bit of leftover cranberry sauce.
Perfect for a romaine lettuce salad with turkey or chicken.

Cooking oil	3 tbsp.	50 mL
Jellied cranberry sauce	2 tbsp.	30 mL
White wine vinegar	1 1/2 tbsp.	25 mL
Dijon mustard	1 tbsp.	15 mL

Combine all 4 ingredients and a sprinkle of salt and pepper in jar with tight-fitting lid. Shake well. Store in airtight container in refrigerator for up to 1 week. Makes about 1/2 cup (125 mL).

2 tbsp. (30 mL): 105 Calories; 10.2 g Total Fat (5.9 g Mono, 3.1 g Poly, 0.7 g Sat); 0 mg Cholesterol; 4 g Carbohydrate; trace Fibre; 0 g Protein; 53 mg Sodium

Paré Pointer

Don't try to shoot a mouse that runs out of your stove.
It's out of your range!

Tomato Pesto Dressing

Add this to a pasta or vegetable salad, or use as a marinade.

Sun-dried tomato pesto	1/3 cup	75 mL
Coarsely chopped fresh parsley	1/3 cup	75 mL
Tomato juice	1/3 cup	75 mL
Red wine vinegar	3 tbsp.	50 mL

Process all 4 ingredients in blender or food processor until smooth. Store in airtight container in refrigerator for up to 1 week. Makes about 3/4 cup (175 mL).

2 tbsp. (30 mL): 18 Calories; 0.9 g Total Fat (0.5 g Mono, 0.1 g Poly, 0.1 g Sat); 0 mg Cholesterol; 3 g Carbohydrate; trace Fibre; 1 g Protein; 68 mg Sodium

Orange Sesame Dressing

A great dressing for a spinach salad or oriental-style coleslaw.

Medium orange	1	1
Oyster sauce	3 tbsp.	50 mL
Rice vinegar	3 tbsp.	50 mL
Sesame oil, for flavour	2 tbsp.	30 mL

Grate 1 tsp. (5 mL) orange zest into small bowl. Squeeze and add 1/4 cup (60 mL) orange juice.

Add remaining 3 ingredients. Stir well. Store in airtight container in refrigerator for up to 1 week. Makes about 2/3 cup (150 mL).

2 tbsp. (30 mL): 74 Calories; 5.1 g Total Fat (2 g Mono, 2.1 g Poly, 0.7 g Sat); 0 mg Cholesterol; 7 g Carbohydrate; trace Fibre; 0 g Protein; 211 mg Sodium

Paré Pointer

A long time salesman joined the police force. He wanted to work where the customer is always wrong.

Creamy Bruschetta Dressing

Puréed bruschetta makes a thick dressing for
any salad, whether green, pasta or vegetable.

Bruschetta topping	1/2 cup	125 mL
Mayonnaise	1/4 cup	60 mL
Chopped fresh basil (or 3/4 tsp., 4 mL, dried)	1 tbsp.	15 mL
Balsamic vinegar	1 tbsp.	15 mL

Process all 4 ingredients in blender or food processor until smooth.
Store in airtight container in refrigerator for up to 1 week. Makes about
1 cup (250 mL).

2 tbsp. (30 mL): 55 Calories; 5.7 g Total Fat (3.1 g Mono, 1.9 g Poly, 0.5 g Sat); 4 mg Cholesterol;
1 g Carbohydrate; trace Fibre; 0 g Protein; 79 mq Sodium

Dijon Chèvre Dressing

Drizzle this tangy, versatile dressing on potato or shrimp
salad, or serve as a sauce to accompany salmon.

Goat (chèvre) cheese, cut up	3 oz.	85 g
Dijon-flavoured mayonnaise	1/3 cup	75 mL
Apple cider vinegar	1 1/2 tbsp.	25 mL
Pepper	1/2 tsp.	2 mL

Put all 4 ingredients into blender or food processor. Add 1/4 cup (60 mL)
water. Process until smooth. Store in airtight container in refrigerator for up
to 1 week. Makes about 1 cup (250 mL).

2 tbsp. (30 mL): 92 Calories; 9.3 g Total Fat (4.6 g Mono, 2.5 g Poly, 2 g Sat); 10 mg Cholesterol;
1 g Carbohydrate; trace Fibre; 1 g Protein; 81 mg Sodium

Four-Cheese Broccoli Soup

Thick, rich, creamy—and ready in no time! Have it for
lunch with some Feta Crescent Swirls, page 22.

Diced onion	1 cup	250 mL
Cans of low-sodium condensed chicken broth (10 oz., 284 mL, each)	2	2
Bag of frozen chopped broccoli, thawed and chopped smaller	16 oz.	455 g
Four-cheese white pasta sauce	1 1/3 cups	325 mL

Heat large greased saucepan on medium. Add onion. Cook for 5 to 10 minutes, stirring often, until softened.

Add remaining 3 ingredients. Stir. Bring to a boil. Reduce heat to medium-low. Simmer, uncovered, for about 8 minutes, stirring occasionally, until broccoli is tender. Cool slightly. Process soup in 2 batches in blender or food processor until smooth (see Safety Tip). Return to same saucepan. Heat and stir on medium until heated through. Makes about 5 1/2 cups (1.4 L).

1 cup (250 mL): 141 Calories; 6.5 g Total Fat (2.4 g Mono, 1.1 g Poly, 2.6 g Sat); 14 mg Cholesterol; 14 g Carbohydrate; 3 g Fibre; 9 g Protein; 951 mg Sodium

Safety Tip: Follow manufacturer's instructions for processing hot liquids.

Sausage And Spinach Soup

A savoury tomato soup laden with sausage, spinach
and herbs. Sure to become a favourite!

Hot Italian sausages	1/2 lb.	225 g
Can of diced tomatoes with roasted garlic and basil (with juice)	19 oz.	540 mL
Can of condensed chicken broth with garlic and herbs	10 oz.	284 mL
Fresh spinach, stems removed, coarsely chopped, lightly packed	3 cups	750 mL

(continued on next page)

Heat medium greased frying pan on medium. Add sausages. Cook for 5 minutes, turning once. Reduce heat to medium-low. Cook for about 15 minutes, turning once or twice, until no longer pink inside. Transfer to paper towels to drain. Cut sausages lengthwise into quarters, then into 1/2 inch (12 mm) pieces. Set aside.

Combine tomatoes with juice, broth and 2 cups (500 mL) water in large saucepan. Heat and stir on medium until boiling. Reduce heat to medium-low. Add sausage. Stir. Simmer, covered, for 5 minutes.

Add spinach and a sprinkle of salt and pepper. Heat and stir until spinach is wilted. Makes about 7 cups (1.75 L).

1 cup (250 mL): 146 Calories; 10.8 g Total Fat (4.9 g Mono, 1.5 g Poly, 3.8 g Sat); 25 mg Cholesterol; 5 g Carbohydrate; 1 g Fibre; 8 g Protein; 652 mg Sodium

Curry Vegetable Soup

A creamy base and chunky vegetables make a colourful soup for a simple lunch or supper.

Envelope of cream of leek soup mix	2 3/4 oz.	77 g
Curry powder	1 tbsp.	15 mL
Frozen mixed vegetables	1 1/2 cups	375 mL
Milk	1 cup	250 mL

Combine soup mix, curry powder and 3 cups (750 mL) water in large saucepan. Bring to a boil, stirring often. Reduce heat to medium-low. Simmer, covered, for 5 minutes. Increase heat to medium.

Add vegetables, milk and a sprinkle of pepper. Stir. Cook for about 8 minutes, stirring occasionally, until vegetables are tender. Makes about 4 cups (1 L).

1 cup (250 mL): 151 Calories; 3.4 g Total Fat (1.1 g Mono, 0.3 g Poly, 1.5 g Sat); 5 mg Cholesterol; 25 g Carbohydrate; 2 g Fibre; 7 g Protein; 1056 mg Sodium

Pictured on page 36.

Simple Seafood Bisque

Sherry provides a subtle sweetness to this creamy combination.

Can of ready-to-serve New England clam chowder	19 oz.	540 mL
Can of condensed tomato soup	10 oz.	284 mL
Can of crabmeat, drained, cartilage removed, flaked	5 oz.	142 g
Medium sherry	2 tbsp.	30 mL

Process chowder in blender or food processor until smooth. Transfer to medium saucepan.

Add soup. Stir. Add crabmeat and 1 cup (250 mL) water. Stir well. Heat on medium-low, stirring often, until boiling. Remove from heat.

Add sherry. Stir. Makes about 4 2/3 cups (1.15 L).

1 cup (250 mL): 148 Calories; 4.4 g Total Fat (1.3 g Mono, 1 g Poly, 1.6 g Sat); 11 mg Cholesterol; 17 g Carbohydrate; 1 g Fibre; 10 g Protein; 1130 mg Sodium

Ginger Squash Soup

Simmered in broth and ginger, tender squash makes an elegant soup.

Garlic-flavoured olive oil	1 tbsp.	15 mL
Butternut (or acorn) squash, cubed	1 lb.	454 g
Coarsely chopped, peeled gingerroot	1 tbsp.	15 mL
Cans of condensed chicken broth (10 oz., 284 mL, each)	2	2

Heat olive oil in large pot or Dutch oven on medium. Add squash and ginger. Cook for about 15 minutes, stirring occasionally, until squash is softened and lightly browned.

Add broth and 2 1/2 cups (625 mL) water. Stir. Bring to a boil. Reduce heat to medium-low. Simmer, covered, for 20 minutes, stirring occasionally. Remove from heat. Cool slightly. Process soup in 2 batches in blender or food processor until smooth (see Safety Tip). Return to same pot. Sprinkle with salt and pepper. Heat and stir on medium until heated through. Makes about 6 cups (1.5 L).

1 cup (250 mL): 82 Calories; 3.4 g Total Fat (2.2 g Mono, 0.4 g Poly, 0.6 g Sat); 1 mg Cholesterol; 9 g Carbohydrate; 1 g Fibre; 5 g Protein; 632 mg Sodium

Safety Tip: Follow manufacturer's instructions for processing hot liquids.

Thai Chicken Soup

Wow! Fragrant Thai flavours blend with smooth coconut milk in this spicy soup.

Boneless, skinless chicken breast halves, cut into 1/4 inch (6 mm) pieces	12 oz.	340 g
Thai peanut sauce	1/2 cup	125 mL
Boxes of Thai-flavoured broth (16 oz., 500 mL, each), or prepared chicken broth	2	2
Can of light coconut milk	14 oz.	398 mL

Heat large greased frying pan on medium. Add chicken and a sprinkle of salt and pepper. Cook for 5 to 10 minutes, stirring often, until no longer pink.

Add peanut sauce. Heat and stir for about 2 minutes until sauce is slightly thickened.

Add broth and coconut milk. Heat and stir until boiling. Makes about 7 cups (1.75 L).

1 cup (250 mL): 213 Calories; 13.9 g Total Fat (3.7 g Mono, 2.2 g Poly, 6.8 g Sat); 28 mg Cholesterol; 5 g Carbohydrate; 1 g Fibre; 18 g Protein; 822 mg Sodium

Pumpkin Soup

This golden orange soup has a velvety texture. Make some Lemon Poppy Seed Biscuits, page 30, and you're set for dinner!

Medium lime	1	1
Can of pumpkin pie filling	19 oz.	540 mL
Ground cumin	1 tsp.	5 mL
Can of evaporated milk	6 oz.	170 mL

Grate 1 tsp. (5 mL) lime zest for garnish. Set aside. Squeeze and measure 3 tbsp. (50 mL) lime juice into medium saucepan.

Add remaining 3 ingredients and 1 1/2 cups (375 mL) water. Sprinkle with salt and pepper. Stir. Heat on medium, stirring occasionally, until heated through. Garnish individual servings with lime zest. Makes about 5 cups (1.25 L).

1 cup (250 mL): 182 Calories; 3.1 g Total Fat (0.9 g Mono, 0.1 g Poly, 1.8 g Sat); 11 mg Cholesterol; 37 g Carbohydrate; trace Fibre; 4 g Protein; 296 mg Sodium

Pictured on page 108.

Soups

Shortcut Borscht

Sweet and tangy beet broth is complemented by subtle dill.
Easy to prepare, but tastes like you've been cooking all day.

Prepared beef broth	2 cups	500 mL
Dill weed	1 tsp.	5 mL
Can of diced beets in Harvard sauce	14 oz.	398 mL
Coleslaw mix	1 cup	250 mL

Combine broth, dill and 2 cups (500 mL) water in large saucepan. Heat on medium until boiling.

Add beets with sauce, coleslaw mix and a sprinkle of salt and pepper. Stir. Return to a boil. Boil gently, uncovered, for about 8 minutes, stirring occasionally, until vegetables are softened. Makes about 6 cups (1.5 L).

1 cup (250 mL): 60 Calories; 0.3 g Total Fat (0.1 g Mono, 0 g Poly, 0.1 g Sat); 0 mg Cholesterol; 13 g Carbohydrate; 2 g Fibre; 2 g Protein; 390 mg Sodium

Curry Noodle Bowl

A hearty meal in a bowl! Generous portions of tender
noodles and vegetables in a mild curry broth.

Packages of instant noodles with mushroom or vegetable-flavoured seasoning packet (3 oz., 85 g, each)	2	2
Prepared vegetable broth	4 cups	1 L
Red curry paste	1 tbsp.	15 mL
Fresh stir-fry vegetable mix	4 cups	1 L

Break up noodles into medium bowl. Set aside. Combine seasoning packets, broth and curry paste in large saucepan. Add 2 cups (500 mL) water. Stir. Bring to a boil on high.

Add noodles and vegetables. Stir. Cook for about 3 minutes, stirring occasionally, until noodles are tender but firm and vegetables are tender-crisp. Serves 6.

1 serving: 150 Calories; 2.8 g Total Fat (1 g Mono, 0.7 g Poly, 0.6 g Sat); 27 mg Cholesterol; 25 g Carbohydrate; 2 g Fibre; 8 g Protein; 900 mg Sodium

Pictured on front cover.

Salmon-Sauced Bennies

A twist on eggs Benedict that's on the table in no time!
You'll love the rich taste of the smoked salmon sauce.

Smoked salmon spreadable cream cheese	1/2 cup	125 mL
Dill weed	1/4 tsp.	1 mL
Large eggs	8	8
Whole wheat English muffins, split and toasted	4	4

Combine cream cheese, dill and 2 tbsp. (30 mL) water in small saucepan. Heat and stir on medium-low until smooth. Reduce heat to low. Stir occasionally.

Pour water into large frying pan until 1 1/2 to 2 inches (3.8 to 5 cm) deep. Bring to a boil. Reduce heat to medium-low. Water should continue to simmer (see Note). Break 1 egg into shallow dish. Slip egg into water. Repeat with remaining eggs. Cook for about 4 minutes until whites are set and yolks reach desired doneness.

Remove eggs with slotted spoon, shaking gently to remove excess water. Place on muffin halves. Spoon cream cheese mixture onto eggs. Serves 4.

1 serving: 352 Calories; 17.4 g Total Fat (6 g Mono, 2.1 g Poly, 6.8 g Sat); 450 mg Cholesterol; 29 g Carbohydrate; 4 g Fibre; 21 g Protein; 761 mg Sodium

Pictured on page 53 and on back cover.

Note: To help poached eggs retain their shape, add 1 tsp. (5 mL) white vinegar to the simmering water before adding the eggs.

Maui Oatmeal

A healthy breakfast treat bursting with sweet tropical flavours.

Can of crushed pineapple (with juice)	14 oz.	398 mL
Chopped dried apricot	1/2 cup	125 mL
Medium sweetened coconut	1/2 cup	125 mL
Quick-cooking rolled oats	1 1/2 cups	375 mL

Combine first 3 ingredients in medium saucepan. Add 2 1/2 cups (625 mL) water and a pinch of salt. Heat on medium, stirring occasionally, until boiling.

Add rolled oats. Stir. Reduce heat to medium-low. Heat and stir for about 3 minutes until thickened. Remove from heat. Serve immediately or let stand until desired thickness. Serves 6.

1 serving: 460 Calories; 5.2 g Total Fat (0.9 g Mono, 0.8 g Poly, 2.9 g Sat); 0 mg Cholesterol; 104 g Carbohydrate; 13 g Fibre; 8 g Protein; 34 mg Sodium

Blueberry Cream Pancakes

Plump blueberries pump up pancakes for breakfast.
Cream cheese in the batter makes them even better!

Pancake mix	2 cups	500 mL
Blueberry spreadable cream cheese	1/2 cup	125 mL
Milk	1 1/2 cups	375 mL
Fresh (or frozen) blueberries, approximately	1 cup	250 mL

Measure pancake mix into large bowl. Make a well in centre.

Put cream cheese into small bowl. Slowly add milk, beating constantly with whisk until smooth. Add to well. Stir until just moistened. Batter will be lumpy. Heat large greased frying pan on medium-low. Pour batter into pan, using about 1/4 cup (60 mL) for each pancake.

(continued on next page)

Sprinkle pancakes with a few blueberries. Cook for about 3 minutes until bubbles form on top and edges appear dry. Turn. Cook for about 3 minutes until golden. Remove to large plate. Cover to keep warm. Repeat with remaining ingredients, greasing pan again if necessary to prevent sticking. Makes about 12 pancakes.

1 pancake: 136 Calories; 4.3 g Total Fat (1.6 g Mono, 0.7 g Poly, 1.6 g Sat); 13 mg Cholesterol; 20 g Carbohydrate; 1 g Fibre; 4 g Protein; 366 mg Sodium

Pictured on page 53 and on back cover.

PBJ Ring

Baked with the peanut butter and jam right in it, there's no need to dread the spread of PB and J on the countertops when junior gets hold of this!

Frozen white bread dough, covered and thawed in refrigerator overnight	1	1
Crunchy peanut butter	1/4 cup	60 mL
Berry jam	1/4 cup	60 mL
Hard margarine (or butter), melted	1 tbsp.	15 mL

Roll out dough on lightly floured surface to 6 x 18 inch (15 x 45 cm) rectangle.

Combine peanut butter and jam in small bowl. Spread on dough, leaving 1/2 inch (12 mm) edge. Roll up, jelly-roll style, from 1 long side. Moisten edge with water. Press seam against roll to seal. Shape roll into ring. Pinch ends together to seal. Place, seam-side down, in greased 12 cup (3 L) bundt pan. Cover with greased waxed paper and tea towel. Let stand in oven with light on and door closed for 30 minutes. Bake in 375°F (190°C) oven for about 25 minutes until golden.

Brush with margarine. Let stand in pan for 10 minutes before removing to wire rack to cool. Cuts into 12 pieces.

1 piece: 161 Calories; 5.2 g Total Fat (2.6 g Mono, 1.2 g Poly, 1.1 g Sat); 0 mg Cholesterol; 25 g Carbohydrate; 1 g Fibre; 5 g Protein; 246 mg Sodium

Breakfast Bars

*These healthy bran and blueberry bars can be
individually wrapped and frozen for a carry-along snack.*

Large eggs	2	2
Package of blueberry bran muffin mix	2 lbs.	900 g
Chopped pitted dates	1 cup	250 mL
Chopped pecans, toasted (see Tip, page 21)	1 cup	250 mL

Beat eggs and 2 cups (500 mL) water in large bowl until well combined.
Add muffin mix. Stir until smooth.

Add dates and pecans. Stir well. Spread in greased 9 x 13 inch (22 x 33 cm)
pan. Bake in 350°F (175°C) oven for about 40 minutes until wooden pick
inserted in centre comes out clean. Cuts into 24 bars.

*1 bar: 203 Calories; 8.1 g Total Fat (4.1 g Mono, 2.5 g Poly, 1 g Sat); 18 mg Cholesterol;
30 g Carbohydrate; 1 g Fibre; 3 g Protein; 211 mg Sodium*

Pictured on page 144.

1. Swirled Raisin Braid, page 25
2. Berry Bran Shake, page 56
3. Salmon-Sauced Bennies, page 49
4. Blueberry Cream Pancakes, page 50

Props courtesy of: Danesco Inc.

Baked Berry French Toast

A deliciously different way to prepare French toast.

Tub of berry spreadable cream cheese	8 oz.	250 g
Whole wheat bread slices	12	12
Large eggs	6	6
Milk	1 cup	250 mL

Spread cream cheese on 1 side of 6 bread slices. Cover with remaining slices.

Beat eggs and milk in medium bowl until frothy. Pour just enough egg mixture into well-greased 9 × 13 inch (22 × 33 cm) pan to cover bottom. Arrange sandwiches in pan. Pour remaining egg mixture over top. Bake in 450°F (230°C) oven for about 20 minutes until golden and egg is set. Serves 6.

1 serving: 346 Calories; 18.2 g Total Fat (6.9 g Mono, 2.2 g Poly, 7.2 g Sat); 243 mg Cholesterol; 30 g Carbohydrate; 4 g Fibre; 17 g Protein; 674 mg Sodium

Pictured on page 54.

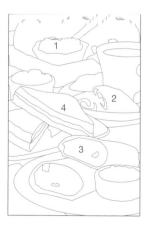

1. Creamy Ginger Spread, page 57
2. Rugalach Roll-Ups, page 26
3. Huevos Tortillas, page 56
4. Baked Berry French Toast, above

Props courtesy of: Casa Bugatti
            Cherison Enterprises Inc.
            Danesco Inc.

Huevos Tortillas

A twist on huevos rancheros, *or "rancher's eggs," these saucy wraps are fun to eat and eggs-tremely quick to make!*

Large eggs	8	8
Chunky medium salsa	1/2 cup	125 mL
Grated Mexican cheese blend (or Cheddar cheese)	1 cup	250 mL
Whole wheat flour tortillas (9 inch, 22 cm, diameter)	4	4

Heat large greased frying pan on medium. Beat eggs and a sprinkle of salt and pepper in medium bowl. Pour into pan. Cook for about 4 minutes, stirring occasionally, until set.

Add salsa. Stir. Remove from heat.

Sprinkle cheese along centre of tortillas. Spoon egg mixture on top of cheese. Fold sides over filling. Roll up tortillas from bottom to enclose. Makes 4 wraps.

1 wrap: 492 Calories; 26.6 g Total Fat (9.7 g Mono, 4 g Poly, 10.2 g Sat); 462 mg Cholesterol; 37 g Carbohydrate; 7 g Fibre; 26 g Protein; 687 mg Sodium

Pictured on page 54.

Berry Bran Shake

Breakfast in a glass! The natural sweetness of fruit gets a boost from raisin bran to make a winning breakfast beverage.

Frozen whole strawberries, cut up	2 cups	500 mL
Milk	2 cups	500 mL
Raisin bran cereal	1/2 cup	125 mL
Chopped pitted dates	1/4 cup	60 mL

Process all 4 ingredients in blender or food processor for about 3 minutes until smooth. Makes about 4 cups (1 L).

1 cup (250 mL): 132 Calories; 1.8 g Total Fat (0.4 g Mono, 0.2 g Poly, 0.9 g Sat); 5 mg Cholesterol; 26 g Carbohydrate; 4 g Fibre; 5 g Protein; 109 mg Sodium

Pictured on page 53 and on back cover.

Creamy Ginger Spread

A delicious cream cheese spread for toasted
multi-grain bread, bagels or banana bread.

Block of cream cheese, softened	8 oz.	250 g
Milk	1 tbsp.	15 mL
Liquid honey	1 tbsp.	15 mL
Minced crystallized ginger	3 tbsp.	50 mL

Beat first 3 ingredients in medium bowl until smooth.

Add ginger. Mix well. Makes about 1 1/4 cups (300 mL).

2 tbsp. (30 mL): 98 Calories; 8.4 g Total Fat (2.4 g Mono, 0.3 g Poly, 5.3 g Sat); 26 mg Cholesterol; 74 g Carbohydrate; 0 g Fibre; 2 g Protein; 73 mg Sodium

Pictured on page 54.

Walnut Pear Dip

You'll go nutty for this cheesy, sweetened dip with a hint of cinnamon.
Serve it on toast or crackers, or with apple and pear slices.

Small pear, peeled and grated	1	1
Goat (chèvre) cheese, cut up and softened	4 oz.	125 g
Finely chopped walnuts, toasted (see Tip, page 21)	2 tbsp.	30 mL
Liquid cinnamon honey	1 tbsp.	15 mL

Beat all 4 ingredients with whisk in medium bowl until well combined. Makes about 1 cup (250 mL).

2 tbsp. (30 mL): 79 Calories; 5.6 g Total Fat (1.3 g Mono, 0.8 g Poly, 3.2 g Sat); 12 mg Cholesterol; 4 g Carbohydrate; trace Fibre; 4 g Protein; 78 mg Sodium

Asiago Soufflé

A perfectly domed, golden soufflé is sure to impress!

Milk	1 1/3 cups	325 mL
Minute tapioca	1/4 cup	60 mL
Grated Asiago cheese	1 cup	250 mL
Large eggs, room temperature	4	4

Preheat oven to 350°F (175°C), see Note. Combine milk, tapioca and a generous sprinkle of salt and pepper in small heavy saucepan. Let stand for 5 minutes. Heat and stir on medium for 8 to 10 minutes until boiling. Remove from heat.

Add cheese. Stir until smooth. Set aside.

Separate eggs, putting whites into medium bowl and yolks into large bowl. Beat egg whites until stiff peaks form. Set aside. Beat egg yolks with same beaters for about 1 minute until frothy. Slowly add cheese mixture to egg yolk, beating constantly on low. Fold in 1/4 of egg white until almost combined. Fold in remaining egg white. Carefully pour into greased 6 cup (1.5 L) soufflé dish (round casserole with high, straight side). Smooth top. Set dish in large roasting pan. Slowly pour enough boiling water into pan until water comes halfway up dish. Bake for about 40 minutes, without opening oven door, until soufflé is puffed and top is golden. Serve immediately. Serves 6.

1 serving: 167 Calories; 9.6 g Total Fat (3.3 g Mono, 0.9 g Poly, 4.6 g Sat); 164 mg Cholesterol; 10 g Carbohydrate; trace Fibre; 10 g Protein; 153 mg Sodium

Note: A preheated oven helps to ensure that a soufflé rises successfully. Once the soufflé is prepared, immediately place it in the hot oven to help preserve its "breath."

Sweet Yam Quesadillas

So good! Serve with sour cream or salsa for dipping.

Yams (or sweet potatoes), peeled and diced	3 1/4 lbs.	1.5 kg
Flour tortillas (9 inch, 22 cm, diameter)	8	8
Grated jalapeño Monterey Jack cheese	2 2/3 cups	650 mL
Can of sliced pickled jalapeño peppers, drained and chopped	4 oz.	114 mL

(continued on next page)

Cook yam in boiling salted water in large saucepan until tender. Drain. Add a sprinkle of salt and pepper. Mash.

Spread mashed yam on tortillas. Sprinkle cheese and jalapeño pepper on half of each tortilla. Fold tortillas in half over filling. Press down lightly. Brush both sides with cooking oil. Arrange on ungreased baking sheets. Bake in 400°F (205°C) oven for about 15 minutes, turning over at halftime, until browned and cheese is melted. Cut each quesadilla into 4 wedges, for a total of 32 wedges. Serves 8.

1 serving: 553 Calories; 18.9 g Total Fat (6.6 g Mono, 2.8 g Poly, 8.5 g Sat); 35 mg Cholesterol; 78 g Carbohydrate; 8 g Fibre; 18 g Protein; 611 mg Sodium

---

Cacciatore Sandwiches

Yum! These hearty open-face sandwiches are great for a hot lunch. Cut the bread diagonally for a touch of class.

Boneless, skinless chicken breast halves, cut into 1 inch (2.5 cm) pieces	1 lb.	454 g
Chunky vegetable pasta sauce	2 cups	500 mL
French bread slices (1 inch, 2.5 cm, thick)	4	4
Grated Italian cheese blend (or mozzarella cheese)	1 cup	250 mL

Heat large greased frying pan on medium. Add chicken. Cook for about 10 minutes, stirring occasionally, until no longer pink inside.

Add pasta sauce and a sprinkle of pepper. Stir. Reduce heat to medium low. Cook, covered, for 10 minutes, stirring occasionally.

Arrange bread slices in ungreased 9 x 13 inch (22 x 33 cm) pan. Broil on centre rack in oven for about 1 minute per side until toasted. Spoon chicken mixture onto toast slices.

Sprinkle with cheese. Broil for another 1 to 2 minutes until cheese is melted and bubbling. Serves 4.

1 serving: 473 Calories; 18.3 g Total Fat (7.5 g Mono, 3.3 g Poly, 5.9 g Sat); 90 mg Cholesterol; 40 g Carbohydrate; 3 g Fibre; 37 g Protein; 982 mg Sodium

Havarti Ham Ring

The enticing combination of cheese, dill, ham and onion spills out of this ring of buttery crescent-roll pastry. Looks lovely on a lunch buffet.

Tubes of refrigerator crescent-style rolls (8 rolls per tube), 8 1/2 oz. (235 g), each	2	2
Grated havarti cheese with dill	1 1/2 cups	375 mL
Finely chopped Black Forest ham	2/3 cup	150 mL
Finely chopped green onion	3 tbsp.	50 mL

Unroll tubes of dough side by side on lightly floured surface, overlapping about 1 inch (2.5 cm). Press perforations and overlapping seam to seal.

Sprinkle cheese over dough, leaving 1/2 inch (12 mm) edge. Scatter ham and onion over cheese. Roll up, jelly-roll style, from 1 long side. Moisten edge with water. Press seam against roll to seal. Place roll, seam-side down, on greased baking sheet. Shape roll into ring. Pinch ends together to seal. Gently stretch ring to 10 inch (25 cm) diameter. Using scissors, make 12 evenly spaced cuts around ring from outside edge to within 1 inch (2.5 cm) of inside edge. Gently turn pieces onto sides in same direction. Pieces will overlap. Bake in 350°F (175°C) oven for about 25 minutes until golden. Let stand for 10 minutes. Cuts into 12 pieces.

1 piece: 133 Calories; 8.3 g Total Fat (1.7 g Mono, 0.4 g Poly, 2.7 g Sat); 19 mg Cholesterol; 8 g Carbohydrate; trace Fibre; 6 g Protein; 421 mg Sodium

Sausage Pandowdy

Pandowdy is usually a deep-dish dessert with sliced apples under a crisp biscuit batter. This is a savoury version with sweet apples and cinnamon that go naturally with pork sausage.

Maple-flavoured pork breakfast sausages	14 oz.	375 g
Chopped onion	1/2 cup	125 mL
Can of apple pie filling	19 oz.	540 mL
Tube of refrigerator crescent-style rolls (8 rolls per tube)	8 1/2 oz.	235 g

(continued on next page)

Lunch

Cook sausages in large greased frying pan on medium for 8 to 10 minutes, turning occasionally, until no longer pink inside. Transfer with slotted spoon to paper towels to drain. Reserve 1 tsp. (5 mL) drippings in pan. Cut sausage into 1/2 inch (12 mm) pieces.

Heat drippings on medium. Add onion. Cook for about 5 minutes, stirring often, until softened.

Add sausage and pie filling. Stir. Spread in greased 9 x 9 inch (22 x 22 cm) baking dish.

Unroll dough. Separate into triangles. Cut triangles in half. Arrange on top of apple mixture, overlapping if necessary. Bake, uncovered, in 350°F (175°C) oven for about 25 minutes until top is crisp and golden. Let stand for 5 minutes. Serves 4.

1 serving: 377 Calories; 15 g Total Fat (4.5 g Mono, 1.3 g Poly, 3.6 g Sat); 37 mg Cholesterol; 53 g Carbohydrate; 2 g Fibre; 9 g Protein; 692 mg Sodium

---

Chicken And Cheese Pizza

When you have leftover chicken, make this quick and easy lunch.
Enough for one, or serve two by adding soup on the side.

Whole wheat flour tortilla (9 inch, 22 cm, diameter)	1	1
Mild salsa	2 tbsp.	30 mL
Finely chopped cooked chicken	1/2 cup	125 mL
Grated medium Cheddar cheese	1/4 cup	60 mL

Place tortilla on greased baking sheet or 12 inch (30 cm) pizza pan. Spread salsa on tortilla, almost to edge.

Scatter chicken over salsa. Sprinkle with cheese. Bake on bottom rack in 375°F (190°C) oven for about 15 minutes until tortilla is crisp and cheese is melted. Cuts into 6 wedges.

1 wedge: 82 Calories; 3.5 g Total Fat (1.2 g Mono, 0.6 g Poly, 1.5 g Sat); 19 mg Cholesterol; 6 g Carbohydrate; 6 g Fibre; 7 g Protein; 106 mg Sodium

Seafood Quesadillas

When you're expecting a bunch for lunch, serve these seafood quesadillas filled with sweet baby shrimp and creamy cheese. Sure to fill the bill!

Tub of smoked salmon spreadable cream cheese	8 oz.	250 g
Flour tortillas (9 inch, 22 cm, diameter)	8	8
Grated jalapeño Monterey Jack cheese	2 cups	500 mL
Frozen cooked baby shrimp, thawed and blotted dry	2 cups	500 mL

Spread cream cheese on tortillas. Sprinkle Monterey Jack cheese and shrimp over half of each tortilla. Fold tortillas in half over filling. Press down lightly. Brush both sides with cooking oil. Place on ungreased baking sheets. Bake in 400°F (205°C) oven for about 15 minutes until cheese is melted. Cut each quesadilla into 4 wedges, for a total of 32 wedges. Serves 8.

1 serving: 430 Calories; 22 g Total Fat (7.6 g Mono, 3 g Poly, 10.1 g Sat); 112 mg Cholesterol; 35 g Carbohydrate; 2 g Fibre; 22 g Protein; 740 mg Sodium

Hotsy Totsy Casserole

A tasty lunch dish to please the whole family. Potato tots make this casserole simple to put together.

Plain bratwurst sausages, casings removed, chopped	1 lb.	454 g
Can of condensed cream of mushroom soup, divided	10 oz.	284 mL
Frozen peas	1 cup	250 mL
Frozen potato tots (gems or puffs), thawed	4 cups	1 L

(continued on next page)

Scramble-fry sausage in large greased frying pan on medium for about 10 minutes until no longer pink. Transfer to paper towels to drain.

Put 1/2 of soup in medium bowl. Add sausage. Stir. Spread in ungreased 9 x 9 inch (22 x 22 cm) baking dish.

Scatter peas over sausage mixture. Arrange potato tots on top. Combine remaining soup and 1/3 cup (75 mL) water in small bowl. Drizzle over potato tots. Bake, uncovered, in 350°F (175°C) oven for about 1 hour until golden. Serves 4.

1 serving: 482 Calories; 27.3 g Total Fat (10.5 g Mono, 4.7 g Poly, 10.6 g Sat); 33 mg Cholesterol; 44 g Carbohydrate; 5 g Fibre; 14 g Protein; 1730 mg Sodium

Feta Shrimp Frittata

A golden-topped, fluffy frittata filled with savoury cheeses and tender shrimp. Lovely served with pasta or a green salad.

Large eggs	8	8
Herb and garlic spreadable cream cheese	1/4 cup	60 mL
Cooked salad shrimp	12 oz.	340 g
Crumbled feta cheese	1 cup	250 mL

Heat large well-greased frying pan on medium. Beat eggs and cream cheese in medium bowl until smooth.

Add shrimp and feta cheese. Stir. Pour into pan. Stir for 5 seconds. Spread evenly in pan. Reduce heat to medium-low. Cook, covered, for about 8 minutes until bottom is golden and top is almost set. Place pan on centre rack in oven (see Note). Broil for about 5 minutes until frittata is browned and set. Cuts into 4 wedges.

1 wedge: 396 Calories; 25 g Total Fat (8.2 g Mono, 2.8 g Poly, 11.4 g Sat); 643 mg Cholesterol; 3 g Carbohydrate; 0 g Fibre; 38 g Protein; 881 mg Sodium

Note: To avoid damaging the frying pan handle in the oven, wrap the handle with foil before placing under the broiler.

Mexican Meatless Lasagne

You'll never miss the meat! This lasagne delivers a spicy
kick in tasty layers of soft tortillas, tangy sauce
and seasoned, soy-based ground round.

Chunky medium salsa	3 cups	750 mL
Flour tortillas (9 inch, 22 cm, diameter), quartered	4	4
Package of Mexican veggie ground round	12 oz.	340 g
Grated jalapeño Monterey Jack cheese	2 cups	500 mL

Layer all 4 ingredients in greased 8 × 8 inch (20 × 20 cm) pan as follows:

A. 1 cup (250 mL) salsa

B. 8 tortilla quarters, slightly overlapping

C. 1 cup (250 mL) salsa

D. 1/2 of ground round

E. 1 cup (250 mL) cheese

F. 8 tortilla quarters, slightly overlapping

G. 1 cup (250 mL) salsa

H. 1/2 of ground round

I. 1 cup (250 mL) cheese

Bake, covered with greased foil, in 350°F (175°C) oven for about 50 minutes until heated through. Broil, uncovered, on centre rack for about 5 minutes until cheese is golden. Let stand for about 10 minutes until set. Serves 6.

1 serving: 368 Calories; 15.3 g Total Fat (4.7 g Mono, 1.7 g Poly, 8.1 g Sat); 35 mg Cholesterol; 34 g Carbohydrate; 4 g Fibre; 25 g Protein; 1034 mg Sodium

Pictured on page 90.

Polenta Lasagne

Make lunch time fiesta time! Polenta goes well with
Mexican seasonings and tomato. Definitely one to try.

Chunky salsa	2 cups	500 mL
Package of veggie ground round	12 oz.	340 g
Polenta roll, cut into 24 slices	2 1/4 lbs.	1 kg
Grated jalapeño Monterey Jack cheese	2 cups	500 mL

Combine salsa and ground round in large bowl. Spread 1/3 of salsa mixture in greased 9 × 13 inch (22 × 33 cm) baking dish.

Arrange 12 polenta slices on salsa mixture. Spread another 1/3 of salsa mixture on top of polenta. Sprinkle with 1/2 of cheese. Layer with remaining polenta slices, salsa mixture and cheese, in order given. Bake, uncovered, in 350°F (175°C) oven for about 45 minutes until cheese is melted and polenta is softened. Serves 6.

1 serving: 368 Calories; 14.3 g Total Fat (4.4 g Mono, 1 g Poly, 7.7 g Sat); 35 mg Cholesterol; 37 g Carbohydrate; 2 g Fibre; 24 g Protein; 725 mg Sodium

Salsa Bean Cakes

Healthy corn and bean cakes are crisp on the outside and soft in the
middle. Serve on hamburger buns with your favourite toppings.

Can of red kidney beans, rinsed and drained	19 oz.	540 mL
Crushed corn tortilla chips	1 cup	250 mL
Medium salsa	1/2 cup	125 mL
Large egg, fork-beaten	1	1

Mash beans with a fork in medium bowl.

Add remaining 3 ingredients. Stir well. Shape into 6 patties to fit buns. Heat large greased frying pan on medium. Add patties. Cook for about 5 minutes per side until browned and heated through. Serves 6.

1 serving: 142 Calories; 5.7 g Total Fat (3 g Mono, 1.1 g Poly, 1 g Sat); 36 mg Cholesterol; 18 g Carbohydrate; 4 g Fibre; 6 g Protein; 231 mg Sodium

Pictured on page 90.

Meat And Potato Scallop

A satisfying, homestyle casserole that's a snap to put together.

Lean ground beef	1 lb.	454 g
Can of condensed cream of mushroom soup	10 oz.	284 mL
Thinly sliced peeled potato	4 cups	1 L
Thinly sliced onion	1 cup	250 mL

Scramble-fry ground beef in large greased frying pan on medium for about 10 minutes until no longer pink. Drain. Sprinkle with salt and pepper. Stir. Spread in ungreased 2 quart (2 L) casserole.

Combine soup and 3/4 cup (175 mL) water in large bowl. Add potato, onion and a sprinkle of salt and pepper. Stir. Spoon onto beef. Bake, covered, in 350°F (175°C) oven for 1 hour. Bake, uncovered, for another 10 to 15 minutes until top is starting to brown and potato is tender. Serves 4.

1 serving: 391 Calories; 15.3 g Total Fat (5.2 g Mono, 3.1 g Poly, 5.3 g Sat); 59 mg Cholesterol; 38 g Carbohydrate; 3 g Fibre; 25 g Protein; 664 mg Sodium

Quickest Chili

It doesn't get much quicker than this! A simple one-dish meal solution.

Lean ground beef	1 lb.	454 g
Frozen mixed vegetables	2 cups	500 mL
Chili powder	1 tbsp.	15 mL
Cans of baked beans in tomato sauce (14 oz., 398 mL, each)	2	2

Scramble-fry ground beef in large greased frying pan on medium for about 10 minutes until no longer pink. Drain. Sprinkle with salt and pepper. Stir.

(continued on next page)

Add vegetables, chili powder and 1/2 cup (125 mL) water. Heat and stir for 2 minutes.

Add beans. Stir. Reduce heat to medium-low. Cook, uncovered, for 15 minutes, stirring occasionally. Serves 4.

1 serving: 438 Calories; 11.2 g Total Fat (4.2 g Mono, 1 g Poly, 4 g Sat); 59 mg Cholesterol; 58 g Carbohydrate; 20 g Fibre; 34 g Protein; 956 mg Sodium

Barbecued Beef Ribs

Sink your teeth into these! A dark glaze of zesty orange and subtle hickory coats Texas-sized beef ribs, barbecued to perfection. Use twice as much horseradish for a little extra nip.

Beef back ribs, bone-in, cut into 1-bone portions	4 lbs.	1.8 kg
Medium orange	1	1
Hickory barbecue sauce	1 cup	250 mL
Prepared horseradish	1 tbsp.	15 mL

Put ribs into large pot or Dutch oven. Cover with water. Add a sprinkle of salt and pepper. Bring to a boil. Reduce heat to medium-low. Simmer, covered, for about 1 1/2 hours until tender. Drain. Sprinkle ribs with salt and pepper. Set aside.

Grate 1 tsp. (5 mL) orange zest into small bowl. Squeeze and add 1/4 cup (60 mL) orange juice. Add barbecue sauce and horseradish. Stir well. Preheat gas barbecue to medium-high. Place ribs on 1 side of greased grill. Turn off burner under ribs, leaving opposite burner on medium high. Brush ribs with sauce. Close lid. Cook for about 25 minutes, turning occasionally and brushing with remaining sauce, until ribs are browned and glazed. Serves 6.

1 serving: 308 Calories; 16.5 g Total Fat (7.2 g Mono, 0.8 g Poly, 6.8 g Sat); 74 mg Cholesterol; 7 g Carbohydrate; 3 g Fibre; 31 g Protein; 418 mg Sodium

Stroganoff

Tender, chunky beef and mushrooms in a rich, creamy gravy.
Delicious served with egg noodles or mashed potatoes.

Beef stew meat, cut into 3/4 inch (2 cm) cubes	1 1/2 lbs.	680 g
Sliced fresh white mushrooms	3 cups	750 mL
Envelope of cream of mushroom soup mix	2 1/2 oz.	71 g
Sour cream	1/2 cup	125 mL

Heat large well-greased frying pan or Dutch oven on medium-high. Add beef. Cook for about 10 minutes, stirring occasionally, until browned.

Add mushrooms and a sprinkle of pepper. Cook for about 5 minutes, stirring occasionally, until mushrooms are softened.

Add soup mix. Stir. Slowly add 3 cups (750 mL) water, stirring constantly. Bring to a boil. Reduce heat to medium-low. Simmer, covered, for about 1 1/2 hours, stirring occasionally, until beef is tender.

Add sour cream and another sprinkle of pepper. Heat and stir for 2 to 3 minutes until heated through. Serves 6.

1 serving: 298 Calories; 16.9 g Total Fat (7.1 g Mono, 1.9 g Poly, 6.3 g Sat); 71 mg Cholesterol; 9 g Carbohydrate; trace Fibre; 27 g Protein; 631 mg Sodium

Chutney Steak

Try this tender steak smothered in a sweet, tasty sauce.
Add rice and a salad, and dinner is served!

Boneless beef blade steak, cut into 4 equal pieces	1 lb.	454 g
Prepared beef broth	1 cup	250 mL
Mango chutney, larger pieces chopped	1/2 cup	125 mL
Dijon mustard	3 tbsp.	50 mL

(continued on next page)

Heat medium greased frying pan on medium. Sprinkle both sides of steak pieces with salt and pepper. Add to pan. Cook for about 5 minutes per side until browned.

Combine remaining 3 ingredients in small bowl. Pour over steak. Bring to a boil. Reduce heat to medium-low. Simmer, covered, for about 1 hour until steak is tender. Remove steak to large serving platter. Cover to keep warm. Increase heat to medium. Cook sauce for 2 to 3 minutes, stirring occasionally, until thickened. Skim any fat from surface. Pour sauce over steak. Serves 4.

1 serving: 316 Calories; 21.5 g Total Fat (9.4 g Mono, 1.5 g Poly, 8.1 g Sat); 67 mg Cholesterol; 9 g Carbohydrate; trace Fibre; 21 g Protein; 439 mg Sodium

Easy Pot Roast

The name says it all! Tender beef and vegetables are wonderfully flavoured with a tangy sweet sauce in this one-pot meal. Thicken the sauce for gravy if desired.

Boneless blade (or chuck) roast	3 lbs.	1.4 kg
Potatoes, peeled and quartered	2 lbs.	900 g
Medium carrots, halved	4	4
Steak sauce	1 2/3 cups	400 mL

Place roast in medium roasting pan. Sprinkle with pepper.

Arrange potatoes and carrots around roast in pan. Sprinkle with salt and pepper.

Combine steak sauce and 1 1/2 cups (375 mL) water in small bowl. Pour over roast and vegetables. Cook, covered, in 325°F (160°C) oven for about 2 1/4 hours, turning roast twice, until roast and vegetables are very tender. Remove roast to large serving platter. Cover with foil. Let stand for 10 minutes. Remove vegetables with slotted spoon to large serving bowl. Remove sauce to small serving bowl. Cover both to keep warm. Slice roast. Makes 12 servings (2 to 3 oz., 57 to 85 g, each). Serve with vegetables and sauce. Serves 12.

1 serving: 316 Calories; 17.5 g Total Fat (7.4 g Mono, 0.7 g Poly, 6.8 g Sat); 67 mg Cholesterol; 18 g Carbohydrate; 2 g Fibre; 22 g Protein; 593 mg Sodium

Meaty Potato Bake

A great way to use up leftover beef. Just add a
few basic ingredients and supper is underway!

Cubed peeled potato	3 cups	750 mL
Chopped cooked roast beef	2 cups	500 mL
Can of condensed tomato soup	10 oz.	284 mL
Grated sharp Cheddar cheese	1 1/2 cups	375 mL

Combine first 3 ingredients and a sprinkle of pepper in medium bowl.
Spread in greased 2 quart (2 L) casserole. Bake, covered, in 350°F (175°C)
oven for 1 to 1 1/4 hours until potato is tender.

Sprinkle with cheese. Bake, uncovered, for another 2 to 3 minutes until
cheese is melted. Serves 4.

1 serving: 482 Calories; 22.6 g Total Fat (7.1 g Mono, 1.3 g Poly, 12 g Sat); 96 mg Cholesterol;
32 g Carbohydrate; 3 g Fibre; 38 g Protein; 853 mg Sodium

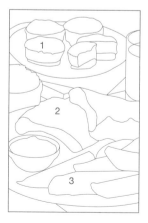

1. Berry Mini-Cheesecakes, page 147
2. Peppered Dry Ribs, page 81
3. Oven Ranch Fries, page 102

Props courtesy of: Cherison Enterprises Inc.

"Sweetish" Meatballs

Convenient to toss together in the slow cooker before running errands for the day. This sweet tomato sauce with tender meatballs can be served over rice.

Can of condensed tomato soup	10 oz.	284 mL
Brown sugar, packed	3/4 cup	175 mL
White vinegar	1/2 cup	125 mL
Package of frozen cooked meatballs	2 1/4 lbs.	1 kg

Combine first 3 ingredients in medium bowl.

Put meatballs into 4 to 5 quart (4 to 5 L) slow cooker. Sprinkle with salt and pepper. Pour soup mixture over meatballs. Stir until coated. Cook, covered, on Low for 5 to 6 hours or on High for 2 1/2 to 3 hours until heated through. Serves 8.

1 serving: 273 Calories; 5.6 g Total Fat (0.1 g Mono, 0.3 g Poly, 0.1 g Sat); 0 mg Cholesterol; 48 g Carbohydrate; trace Fibre; 9 g Protein; 587 mg Sodium

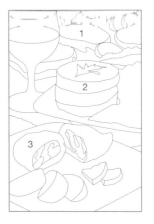

1. Salmon Lime Patties, page 76
2. Salmon-Stuffed Brie, page 15
3. Shrimp-Stuffed Sole, page 75

Props courtesy of: Danesco Inc.
Totally Bamboo

Pepper Steak

Perfectly peppery, and just plain good! A spicy crust adds a spark to tender, juicy steak. Double the peppercorns for added bite!

Whole mixed (or black) peppercorns, crushed (see Tip, page 75)	1 tbsp.	15 mL
Montreal steak spice	2 tsp.	10 mL
Rib-eye (or strip loin) steaks (4 – 6 oz., 113 – 170 g, each)	2	2
Garlic-flavoured olive oil	2 tbsp.	30 mL

Combine peppercorns and steak spice in small cup. Rub on both sides of steaks. Place on large plate.

Drizzle with olive oil. Let stand for 10 minutes. Preheat gas barbecue to medium-high (see Note). Cook steaks on greased grill for about 4 minutes per side for medium-rare, or until desired doneness. Serves 2.

1 serving: 394 Calories; 32.1 g Total Fat (18.1 g Mono, 1.8 g Poly, 9.4 g Sat); 60 mg Cholesterol; 3 g Carbohydrate; 1 g Fibre; 23 g Protein; 1248 mg Sodium

Note: Steaks may be broiled in the oven. Place steaks on a greased broiler pan. Broil on the top rack for about 4 minutes per side for medium-rare, or until desired doneness.

Onion Beef Ragoût

Beef stew was never so simple, or so good. Serve with mashed potatoes and buttered green beans.

Beef stew meat, cut into 3/4 inch (2 cm) cubes	2 lbs.	900 g
Envelope of green peppercorn sauce mix	1 1/4 oz.	38 g
Medium onions, each cut into 8 wedges	3	3
Dry (or alcohol-free) red wine	1/2 cup	125 mL

Put beef into 4 to 5 quart (4 to 5 L) slow cooker. Sprinkle with sauce mix. Toss until coated. Arrange onion wedges on top of beef.

Combine wine and 1 cup (250 mL) water in small bowl. Pour over onion. Cook, covered, on Low for 8 to 9 hours or on High for 4 to 4 1/2 hours until beef is tender. Serves 8.

1 serving: 235 Calories; 10.3 g Total Fat (4.1 g Mono, 0.4 g Poly, 3.9 g Sat); 62 mg Cholesterol; 6 g Carbohydrate; 1 g Fibre; 26 g Protein; 380 mg Sodium

Shrimp-Stuffed Sole

An elegant dish seasoned with mild garlic and herbs.
Perfect for company.

Frozen uncooked shrimp (peeled and deveined), thawed, blotted dry, finely chopped	1 lb.	454 g
Crushed Caesar-flavoured croutons	1 cup	250 mL
Sole fillets (3 – 4 oz., 85 – 113 g, each), any small bones removed	8	8
Garlic butter, melted	1/4 cup	60 mL

Combine shrimp and crushed croutons in medium bowl.

Place sole fillets on work surface. Spoon shrimp mixture onto centre of fillets. Fold 1 end of each fillet over stuffing and roll up. Place, seam-side down, in greased 9 x 13 inch (22 x 33 cm) baking dish.

Drizzle butter over fillets. Bake, uncovered, in 350°F (175°C) oven for 25 to 30 minutes until shrimp turns pink and fish flakes easily when tested with a fork. Serves 8.

1 serving: 211 Calories; 10 g Total Fat (3.3 g Mono, 1.3 g Poly, 4.5 g Sat); 122 mg Cholesterol; 4 g Carbohydrate; trace Fibre; 25 g Protein; 260 mg Sodium

Pictured on page 72.

 tip To crush peppercorns easily and keep them from spilling, place them in a resealable bag. Do not seal the bag. Use a rolling pin to gently pound and roll the peppercorns until crushed.

Creamy Curry Shrimp

Tender curried shrimp with chunks of
tomato—a perfect topping for rice or pasta.

Frozen uncooked large shrimp (peeled and deveined), thawed and blotted dry	1 lb.	454 g
Curry powder	1 tbsp.	15 mL
Can of diced tomatoes (with juice)	14 oz.	398 mL
Sour cream	1/2 cup	125 mL

Put shrimp into large bowl. Sprinkle with curry powder. Stir well. Heat greased wok or large frying pan on medium-high until very hot. Add shrimp. Stir-fry for about 3 minutes until shrimp just start to turn pink. Transfer to medium bowl.

Heat tomatoes with juice in same wok until boiling. Reduce heat to medium. Boil gently, uncovered, for about 6 minutes, stirring occasionally, until liquid is almost evaporated.

Add shrimp and sour cream. Heat and stir for about 3 minutes until sauce is boiling. Serves 4.

1 serving: 182 Calories; 8.5 g Total Fat (2.8 g Mono, 1.5 g Poly, 3.1 g Sat); 141 mg Cholesterol; 7 g Carbohydrate; 1 g Fibre; 19 g Protein; 304 mg Sodium

Salmon Lime Patties

These are a nice change from conventional beef patties.
Try other salmon varieties for a deeper red colour.

Medium lime	1	1
Cans of skinless, boneless pink salmon (6 oz., 170 g, each), drained	2	2
Large egg, fork-beaten	1	1
Crushed seasoned croutons	1 cup	250 mL

(continued on next page)

Grate 1 tsp. (5 mL) lime zest into medium bowl. Squeeze and add 3 tbsp. (50 mL) lime juice.

Add remaining 3 ingredients and a sprinkle of salt and pepper. Mix well. Shape into six 1/2 inch (12 mm) thick patties. Heat large well-greased frying pan on medium. Add patties. Cook for about 3 minutes per side until browned and heated through. Serves 6.

1 serving: 136 Calories; 8.1 g Total Fat (3.7 g Mono, 2.3 g Poly, 1.6 g Sat); 48 mg Cholesterol; 5 g Carbohydrate; trace Fibre; 10 g Protein; 332 mg Sodium

Pictured on page 72.

Lemon Tuna Fettuccine

Fresh lemon and garlic make tuna fish taste tuna-rrific!

Spinach fettuccine	13 oz.	370 g
Garlic butter, softened	1/4 cup	60 mL
Medium lemon	1	1
Can of white tuna in water, drained and broken up	6 1/2 oz.	184 g

Cook fettuccine in boiling salted water in large uncovered pot or Dutch oven for 8 to 10 minutes, stirring occasionally, until tender but firm. Drain. Return to same pot.

Add butter and a sprinkle of salt and pepper. Stir until butter is melted.

Grate 2 tsp. (10 mL) lemon zest into small bowl. Squeeze and add 2 tbsp. (30 mL) lemon juice. Stir. Add to fettuccine. Toss. Add tuna. Toss well. Serves 4.

1 serving: 509 Calories; 14.9 g Total Fat (4 g Mono, 1.5 g Poly, 8.2 g Sat); 49 mg Cholesterol; 71 g Carbohydrate; 7 g Fibre; 22 g Protein; 304 mg Sodium

Baked Garlic Shrimp

A garlic-lover's delight! Sherry and garlic butter are drizzled over tender shrimp.
Try these with white wine instead of sherry for a different flavour.

White bread slices, processed into crumbs	4	4
Garlic butter	1/3 cup	75 mL
Frozen uncooked large shrimp (peeled and deveined), thawed and blotted dry	1 lb.	454 g
Dry sherry	2 tbsp.	30 mL

Put bread crumbs into small bowl. Melt butter in small saucepan. Add
3 tbsp. (50 mL) butter and a sprinkle of salt and pepper to crumbs. Toss
well. Set aside.

Arrange shrimp in ungreased 9 × 9 inch (22 × 22 cm) baking dish. Add
sherry to remaining butter. Stir well. Drizzle over shrimp. Sprinkle with
crumb mixture. Bake, uncovered, in 325°F (160°C) oven for about
25 minutes until shrimp are pink and curled. Serves 4.

1 serving: 305 Calories; 18.5 g Total Fat (5.3 g Mono, 1.4 g Poly, 10.5 g Sat); 173 mg Cholesterol;
13 g Carbohydrate; 1 g Fibre; 20 g Protein; 425 mg Sodium

Apricot Wasabi Salmon

An elegant entrée for company. A spicy topping of creamy
mayonnaise goes perfectly with this apricot-glazed salmon.

WASABI MAYONNAISE		
Mayonnaise	1/2 cup	125 mL
Wasabi paste (Japanese horseradish)	2 tsp.	10 mL
Fresh (or frozen, thawed) salmon fillets, skin removed	1 lb.	454 g
Apricot jam	3 tbsp.	50 mL

(continued on next page)

Wasabi Mayonnaise: Combine mayonnaise and wasabi paste in small bowl. Chill for at least 10 minutes to blend flavours. Makes about 1/2 cup (125 mL) mayonnaise.

Arrange fillets on greased baking sheet with sides. Microwave jam in microwave-safe cup on high (100%) for about 30 seconds until melted. Brush on fillets. Sprinkle with salt and pepper. Broil on top rack in oven for about 8 minutes until fish flakes easily when tested with a fork. Serve with Wasabi Mayonnaise. Serves 4.

1 serving: 412 Calories; 30.6 g Total Fat (15.4 g Mono, 10.7 g Poly, 3.3 g Sat); 80 mg Cholesterol; 10 g Carbohydrate; trace Fibre; 23 g Protein; 209 mg Sodium

Zippy Mustard Cod

Reel 'em in for dinner with this one! Mustard and horseradish add zip to this golden, crumb-coated white fish.

Cod fillets, any small bones removed, cut into 4 equal pieces	1 lb.	454 g
Dijon-flavoured mayonnaise	3 tbsp.	50 mL
Prepared horseradish	1 tsp.	5 mL
Crushed seasoned croutons	2/3 cup	150 mL

Arrange fish pieces on greased baking sheet with sides. Sprinkle with salt and pepper.

Combine mayonnaise and horseradish in small cup. Spread on fish. Sprinkle with crushed croutons. Bake in 400°F (205°C) oven for about 15 minutes until fish flakes easily when tested with a fork. Serves 4.

1 serving: 191 Calories; 9.1 g Total Fat (4.6 g Mono, 2.8 g Poly, 1.2 g Sat); 54 mg Cholesterol; 5 g Carbohydrate; trace Fibre; 21 g Protein; 238 mg Sodium

Orange Garlic Fish Fillets

*Sweet, buttery onion with a mild orange flavour enhances the taste
of moist, flaky white fish. A great dish for the supper rush.*

White fish (such as cod or sole) fillets, any small bones removed, cut into 4 equal pieces	1 lb.	454 g
Garlic butter	1 tbsp.	15 mL
Finely chopped onion	1/3 cup	75 mL
Orange juice	3 tbsp.	50 mL

Arrange fish pieces in greased 8 × 8 inch (20 × 20 cm) baking dish. Set aside.

Melt butter in small frying pan on medium. Add onion. Cook for about 5 minutes, stirring often, until softened. Remove from heat.

Add orange juice and a sprinkle of salt and pepper. Stir. Spoon onto fish. Bake, uncovered, in 450°F (230°C) oven for about 10 minutes until fish flakes easily when tested with a fork. Serves 4.

1 serving: 240 Calories; 15.5 g Total Fat (4.8 g Mono, 2.8 g Poly, 6.5 g Sat); 92 mg Cholesterol; 2 g Carbohydrate; trace Fibre; 22 g Protein; 148 mg Sodium

 To store fish, wrap loosely and keep in refrigerator. Cook within 24 hours of purchase. Fish wrapped and stored in the freezer will keep for 2 to 3 months.

Glazed Ham Steak

Sweet and tangy mustard sauce livens up smoky ham. Ready in minutes.

Redcurrant jelly	1/3 cup	75 mL
Prepared horseradish	2 tsp.	10 mL
Dijon mustard (with whole seeds)	2 tsp.	10 mL
Ham steak, rind removed, cut into 6 equal pieces	1 1/2 lbs.	680 g

Combine first 3 ingredients in small cup.

Place ham pieces on greased baking sheet. Spread jelly mixture on ham. Broil on top rack in oven for about 8 minutes until heated through and jelly mixture is bubbling. Serves 6.

1 serving: 165 Calories; 5 g Total Fat (2.2 g Mono, 0.6 g Poly, 1.7 g Sat), 51 mg Cholesterol; 7 g Carbohydrate; trace Fibre; 22 g Protein; 1471 mg Sodium

Peppered Dry Ribs

A first-rate feast! These barbecued, lemony-spiced ribs are a savoury solution for a summer supper.

Lemon pepper	1 tbsp.	15 mL
Cajun seasoning	1 1/2 tsp.	7 mL
Brown sugar, packed	1 1/2 tsp.	7 mL
Baby back pork ribs (about 2 racks)	2 1/2 – 3 lbs.	1.1 – 1.4 kg

Combine first 3 ingredients in small bowl. Rub on both sides of ribs. Preheat gas barbecue to medium-high. Turn off burner on 1 side. Place ribs on greased grill over drip pan on unlit side, leaving opposite burner on medium-high. Close lid. Cook for about 45 minutes, turning occasionally, until tender. Cut into 3-bone portions. Serves 4.

1 serving: 519 Calories; 40.7 g Total Fat (18.4 g Mono, 3.2 g Poly, 15.1 g Sat); 162 mg Cholesterol; 3 g Carbohydrate; trace Fibre; 33 g Protein; 769 mg Sodium

Pictured on page 71.

Pork Chops Normandy

A tasty combination for the slow cooker! The peppery, sweet
applesauce is perfect over noodles, rice or mashed potatoes.

Medium cooking apples (such as McIntosh), peeled and quartered	3	3
Boneless pork loin chops (about 1 1/2 lbs., 680 g), trimmed of fat	6	6
Can of condensed cream of mushroom soup	10 oz.	284 mL
Envelope of green peppercorn sauce mix	1 1/4 oz.	38 g

Put apple into 4 to 5 quart (4 to 5 L) slow cooker. Arrange pork chops on top of apple.

Combine soup, sauce mix and 1 1/2 cups (375 mL) water in medium bowl. Pour over chops. Cover. Cook on Low for 8 to 10 hours or on High for 4 to 5 hours until chops are very tender. Remove chops to large serving platter. Process sauce, in slow cooker with hand blender or in blender or food processor, until smooth. Serve with chops. Serves 6.

1 serving: 242 Calories; 9.7 g Total Fat (3 g Mono, 2.4 g Poly, 2.8 g Sat); 52 mg Cholesterol; 16 g Carbohydrate; 1 g Fibre; 22 g Protein; 864 mg Sodium

Celery-Sauced Chops

Seasoned pork chops with lots of sauce for the potatoes.
Add a vegetable or salad, and dinner's complete!

Red baby potatoes, larger ones cut in half	2 lbs.	900 g
Boneless pork loin chops (about 1 1/2 lbs., 680 g), trimmed of fat	6	6
Montreal chicken spice	1/2 – 1 tsp.	2 – 5 mL
Cans of condensed cream of celery soup (10 oz., 284 mL, each)	2	2

(continued on next page)

Put potatoes into 4 to 5 quart (4 to 5 L) slow cooker. Sprinkle with salt and pepper.

Arrange pork chops on top of potatoes. Sprinkle with chicken spice and a pinch of pepper.

Combine soup and 1 can of water in medium bowl. Pour over chops. Cover. Cook on Low for 8 to 10 hours or on High for 4 to 5 hours. Remove chops and potatoes to large serving platter. Process sauce, in slow cooker with hand blender or in blender or food processor, until smooth (see Safety Tip). Serve with chops and potatoes. Serves 6.

1 serving: 393 Calories; 16.9 g Total Fat (6.5 g Mono, 3.4 g Poly, 5.4 g Sat); 77 mg Cholesterol; 32 g Carbohydrate; 3 g Fibre; 28 g Protein; 869 mg Sodium

Safety Tip: Follow manufacturer's instructions for processing hot liquids.

Perogy Ham Casserole

Smoky ham and melted cheese smother tender perogies. A comforting casserole that holds its heat well, making this a great potluck choice!

Bag of frozen cheese perogies	2 1/4 lbs.	1 kg
Can of condensed cream of mushroom soup	10 oz.	284 mL
Cubed cooked ham	2 cups	500 mL
Grated medium Cheddar cheese	2 cups	500 mL

Cook perogies in boiling water in large pot or Dutch oven for about 5 minutes until tender. Transfer with slotted spoon to well-greased 9 x 13 inch (22 x 33 cm) baking dish.

Combine soup and 3/4 cup (175 mL) water in small bowl. Pour over perogies. Stir gently until coated. Scatter ham over top. Bake, covered with foil, in 350°F (175°C) oven for about 30 minutes until heated through.

Sprinkle with cheese. Bake, uncovered, for another 12 to 15 minutes until cheese is bubbling. Serves 6.

1 serving: 600 Calories; 27.1 g Total Fat (8.4 g Mono, 3 g Poly, 13 g Sat); 96 mg Cholesterol; 55 g Carbohydrate; 5 g Fibre; 33 g Protein; 1238 mg Sodium

Glazed Pork Roast

Sweet, piquant flavours glaze a juicy pork roast.

Redcurrant jelly	1/2 cup	125 mL
Jalapeño jelly	1/4 cup	60 mL
Finely chopped pickled ginger slices	1 tbsp.	15 mL
Boneless pork loin roast	2 1/2 – 3 lbs.	1.1 – 1.4 kg

Combine first 3 ingredients in small bowl. Reserve 1/2 in small serving bowl for dipping sauce.

Place roast in small roasting pan. Score diamond pattern in top of roast. Cook, uncovered, in 400°F (205°C) oven for 30 minutes. Brush 1/2 of jelly mixture on roast. Reduce heat to 325°F (160°C). Cook, uncovered, for about 1 hour, brushing twice with remaining jelly mixture, until meat thermometer inserted into thickest part of roast reads 155°F (68°C). Remove from oven. Cover loosely with foil. Let stand for 10 minutes. Internal temperature should rise to at least 160°F (71°C). Slice roast. Makes 12 servings (2 to 3 oz., 57 to 85 g, each). Serve with reserved dipping sauce. Serves 12.

1 serving: 173 Calories; 7.3 g Total Fat (3.4 g Mono, 0.5 g Poly, 2.7 g Sat); 50 mg Cholesterol; 8 g Carbohydrate; trace Fibre; 18 g Protein; 33 mg Sodium

Pictured on page 126.

 tip Invest in a silicone brush for basting. As well as being durable and easy to clean, it won't lose bristles as you're brushing on a glaze or marinade.

Cheesy Red Rice

Tangy tomato and smoky ham accent this simple supper.

Cans of diced tomatoes with Italian spices (14 oz., 398 mL, each), with juice	2	2
Diced deli ham	1 1/2 cups	375 mL
Grated sharp Cheddar cheese, divided	3 cups	750 mL
Instant white rice	1 1/2 cups	375 mL

Put tomatoes with juice into large saucepan. Add a sprinkle of pepper. Stir. Heat on medium, stirring occasionally, until boiling.

Add ham and 1/2 of cheese. Stir. Remove from heat.

Add rice. Stir well. Let stand, covered, for 5 minutes. Sprinkle with remaining cheese. Let stand, covered, until cheese is melted. Serves 4.

1 serving: 762 Calories; 33.2 g Total Fat (9.9 g Mono, 1.4 g Poly, 20 g Sat); 120 mg Cholesterol; 75 g Carbohydrate; 2 g Fibre; 40 g Protein; 1908 mg Sodium

Picante Spareribs

Tender, moist ribs topped with onion and salsa. Simple, and full of flavour.

Pork spareribs	4 lbs.	1.8 kg
Montreal chicken spice	2 tsp.	10 mL
Chopped onion	2 cups	500 mL
Medium salsa	1 1/2 cups	375 mL

Cut ribs into serving-size portions. Arrange, meaty-side up, in large roasting pan. Sprinkle with chicken spice.

Scatter onion over ribs. Spoon salsa over top. Bake, covered, in 325°F (160°C) oven for about 2 hours until ribs are very tender. Serves 6.

1 serving: 584 Calories; 40.8 g Total Fat (17.6 g Mono, 3.8 g Poly, 15.4 g Sat); 156 mg Cholesterol; 9 g Carbohydrate; 2 g Fibre; 44 g Protein; 546 mg Sodium

Aloha Pork Roast

Tender, succulent pork is glazed with sweet
pineapple and mustard. A tasty tropical delight!

Honey Dijon mustard	1/4 cup	60 mL
Frozen concentrated pineapple juice, thawed	1/4 cup	60 mL
Soy sauce	1 tbsp.	15 mL
Boneless pork loin roast	3 lbs.	1.4 kg

Combine first 3 ingredients in small bowl. Set aside.

Place roast in large roasting pan. Cook, uncovered, in 400°F (205°C) oven for 30 minutes. Brush 1/2 of mustard mixture on roast. Reduce heat to 325°F (160°C). Cook, uncovered, for about 1 hour, brushing twice with remaining mustard mixture, until meat thermometer inserted into thickest part of roast reads 155°F (68°C). Remove from oven. Cover loosely with foil. Let stand for 10 minutes. Internal temperature should rise to at least 160°F (71°C). Slice roast. Makes 12 servings (2 to 3 oz., 57 to 85 g, each).

1 serving: 190 Calories; 9.1 g Total Fat (4.1 g Mono, 0.8 g Poly, 3.2 g Sat); 60 mg Cholesterol; 3 g Carbohydrate; 0 g Fibre; 23 g Protein; 192 mg Sodium

Sweet Onion Bratwurst

Dark and delicious. Sweet balsamic vinegar and cinnamon
honey take sausages from ordinary to extraordinary!

Plain bratwurst sausages (about 4 oz., 113 g, each)	4	4
Sliced red onion	2 1/2 cups	625 mL
Balsamic vinegar	2 tbsp.	30 mL
Liquid cinnamon honey	2 tbsp.	30 mL

(continued on next page)

Poke sausages in several places with a fork. Place in large saucepan. Add 1 cup (250 mL) water. Bring to a boil. Boil gently, covered, for 5 minutes. Boil, uncovered, for about 10 minutes until liquid is evaporated. Transfer sausages to large plate. Heat well-greased large frying pan on medium. Add sausages. Cook for 5 to 10 minutes, turning occasionally, until browned. Remove to large serving plate. Cover to keep warm.

Add onion to same pan. Cook for 15 to 20 minutes, stirring often, until caramelized.

Add vinegar and honey. Heat and stir for about 1 minute until vinegar is evaporated. Spoon over sausages. Serves 4.

1 serving: 303 Calories; 17.9 g Total Fat (8.8 g Mono, 2.6 g Poly, 5.4 g Sat); 44 mg Cholesterol; 20 g Carbohydrate; 2 g Fibre; 12 g Protein; 416 mg Sodium

---

Snappy Apple Pork

A taste of home that's a snap to make. Apples and stuffing with pork chops—great any day of the week!

Can of apple pie filling	19 oz.	540 mL
Box of chicken stove-top stuffing mix	4 1/4 oz.	120 g
Hard margarine (or butter), cut up	3 tbsp.	50 mL
Bone-in pork chops, trimmed of fat	1 1/4 lbs.	560 g

Spread pie filling in greased 2 quart (2 L) casserole.

Combine seasoning packet from stuffing mix, margarine and 3/4 cup (175 mL) water in large saucepan. Bring to a boil. Remove from heat. Add stuffing. Stir. Let stand, covered, for about 5 minutes until liquid is absorbed. Fluff with a fork. Spoon onto pie filling in casserole.

Heat well-greased large frying pan on medium-high. Add pork chops. Cook for 1 to 2 minutes per side until browned. Arrange on top of stuffing mixture. Bake, covered, in 350°F (175°C) oven for 20 minutes. Bake, uncovered, for another 8 to 10 minutes until meat thermometer inserted into centre of pork chop reads 160°F (71°C). Serves 4.

1 serving: 501 Calories; 17.9 g Total Fat (10.2 g Mono, 2.6 g Poly, 3.9 g Sat); 58 mg Cholesterol; 62 g Carbohydrate; 1 g Fibre; 24 g Protein; 704 mg Sodium

Minted Lamb Chops

Excellent! Minty marinade gently complements barbecued lamb.

Zesty Italian dressing	1/4 cup	60 mL
Mint jelly	1/4 cup	60 mL
Dried crushed chilies	1/2 tsp.	2 mL
Lamb loin chops	1 1/2 lbs.	680 g

Process first 3 ingredients in blender or food processor until smooth. Transfer to large resealable freezer bag.

Add lamb chops. Seal bag. Turn until coated. Marinate in refrigerator for at least 6 hours or overnight, turning occasionally. Discard marinade. Preheat gas barbecue to medium. Cook chops on greased grill for about 6 minutes per side for medium-rare, or until desired doneness. Serves 4.

1 serving: 347 Calories; 26.1 g Total Fat (11.7 g Mono, 3.2 g Poly, 9.3 g Sat); 96 mg Cholesterol; 4 g Carbohydrate; trace Fibre; 23 g Protein; 191 mg Sodium

Pictured on page 89.

1. Feta Crescent Swirls, page 22
2. Minted Lamb Chops, above
3. Greek Beans, page 102

Props courtesy of: Casa Bugatti

Baked Tomato Chops

Pork chops are topped with cream cheese and tomato slices, and baked to perfection!

Montreal chicken spice, divided	2 tbsp.	30 mL
Boneless pork loin chops (about 1 lb., 454 g), trimmed of fat	4	4
Chive and onion spreadable cream cheese	1/4 cup	60 mL
Tomato slices (1/4 inch, 6 mm, thick)	8	8

Reserve 1 1/2 tsp. (7 mL) chicken spice in small cup. Rub remaining spice on both sides of pork chops. Arrange in greased 2 quart (2 L) casserole.

Combine cream cheese and 2 tbsp. (30 mL) water in small bowl. Spread on chops.

Top with tomato slices. Sprinkle with reserved spice. Bake, covered, in 350°F (175°C) oven for about 1 hour until chops are very tender. Serves 4.

1 serving: 181 Calories; 8.1 g Total Fat (3.2 g Mono, 0.7 g Poly, 3.5 g Sat); 61 mg Cholesterol; 4 g Carbohydrate; 1 g Fibre; 22 g Protein; 1043 mg Sodium

1. Mexican Meatless Lasagne, page 64
2. Colourful Couscous, page 118
3. Salsa Bean Cakes, page 65

Props courtesy of: Anchor Hocking Canada
Out of the Fire Studio

Garlic Chicken Pasta

Moist pasta with a full garlic presence. A quick, appealing family meal.

Tri-colour fusilli (or other spiral) pasta	3 cups	750 mL
Can of diced tomatoes with roasted garlic and basil (with juice)	19 oz.	540 mL
Diced cooked chicken	2 cups	500 mL
Creamy Caesar dressing	2/3 cup	150 mL

Cook pasta in boiling salted water in large uncovered pot or Dutch oven for 8 to 10 minutes, stirring occasionally, until tender but firm. Drain. Return to same pot. Cover to keep warm.

Combine remaining 3 ingredients in medium saucepan. Heat and stir on medium for 10 to 12 minutes until heated through. Add to pasta. Toss until coated. Serves 4.

1 serving: 719 Calories; 29.1 g Total Fat (2.6 g Mono, 2.2 g Poly, 5.5 g Sat); 94 mg Cholesterol; 74 g Carbohydrate; 4 g Fibre; 40 g Protein; 870 mg Sodium

Pictured on page 36.

Asian Chicken Stir-Fry

Mild oriental flavours coat vegetables and tender chicken.
Stir-fry can't get much easier! Serve with rice.

Boneless, skinless chicken breast halves, cut into 1 inch (2.5 cm) pieces	1 lb.	454 g
Oyster sauce	1/4 cup	60 mL
Hoisin sauce	2 tbsp.	30 mL
Bag of frozen oriental mixed vegetables	17 1/2 oz.	500 g

Heat well-greased wok or large frying pan on medium-high until very hot. Add chicken. Stir-fry for about 8 minutes until no longer pink inside. Reduce heat to medium.

Add both sauces. Stir-fry for 2 minutes. Add vegetables. Stir. Cook, covered, for 6 to 8 minutes, stirring occasionally, until vegetables are tender-crisp. Serves 4.

1 serving: 229 Calories; 5.9 g Total Fat (2.6 g Mono, 1.6 g Poly, 0.9 g Sat); 66 mg Cholesterol; 16 g Carbohydrate; 2 g Fibre; 28 g Protein; 1227 mg Sodium

Savoury Pineapple Chicken

Pretty pineapple-herb topping adds a sweet, mellow flavour to chicken.
Serve over wild rice, jasmine rice or couscous.

Boneless, skinless chicken breast halves (4 – 6 oz., 113 – 170 g, each)	4	4
Can of crushed pineapple (with juice)	14 oz.	398 mL
Cornstarch	2 tsp.	10 mL
Dried savory	1 1/2 tsp.	7 mL

Heat large greased frying pan on medium. Add chicken breast halves. Sprinkle with salt and pepper. Cook for about 5 minutes per side until browned.

Combine remaining 3 ingredients and a sprinkle of salt and pepper in small bowl. Pour over chicken. Stir, scraping any brown bits from bottom of pan. Reduce heat to medium-low. Cook, covered, for about 10 minutes, stirring occasionally, until sauce is thickened and chicken is no longer pink inside. Serves 4.

1 serving: 246 Calories; 4.8 g Total Fat (1.9 g Mono, 1.3 g Poly, 0.8 g Sat); 81 mg Cholesterol; 18 g Carbohydrate; 1 g Fibre; 32 g Protein; 1 mg Sodium

 Make bulk purchases of fresh boneless chicken breasts, less tender steaks and pork ribs. Divide them into meal portions and place them in freezer bags, along with your favourite marinade. Squeeze the air out of the bags, seal, label and freeze. On busy days, remove a bag to the refrigerator in the morning and voila! You're set to go when you get home.

Chicken Corn Spaghetti

This saucy pasta dish can be ready to serve in short order!

Whole wheat spaghetti	6 oz.	170 g
Can of ready-to-serve chicken corn chowder	19 oz.	540 mL
Diced cooked chicken	1 cup	250 mL
Grated Parmesan cheese, divided	1/2 cup	125 mL

Cook spaghetti in boiling salted water in large uncovered pot or Dutch oven for 8 to 10 minutes, stirring occasionally, until tender but firm. Drain. Return to same pot.

Add chowder, chicken and 1/2 cup (125 mL) water. Stir.

Add 1/2 of Parmesan cheese and a sprinkle of salt and pepper. Stir well. Spread in greased 9 x 9 inch (22 x 22 cm) baking dish. Sprinkle with remaining Parmesan cheese. Bake, uncovered, in 425°F (220°C) oven for 15 to 20 minutes until cheese is golden and sauce is bubbling. Serves 4.

1 serving: 402 Calories; 14 g Total Fat (4.8 g Mono, 2 g Poly, 6 g Sat); 65 mg Cholesterol; 42 g Carbohydrate; 4 g Fibre; 29 g Protein; 872 mg Sodium

 Pasta made from regular or whole wheat flour takes the same time to cook, but the whole wheat variety has a delicious nutty flavour and all that extra fibre.

Chicken Alfredo Pie

Quick comfort food that is lip-smacking good!
You'll love the golden crust on this creamy chicken stew.

Boneless, skinless chicken breast halves, cut into 1 inch (2.5 cm) pieces	1 lb.	454 g
Bag of frozen California vegetable mix, thawed and chopped	2 1/4 lbs.	1 kg
Alfredo pasta sauce	1 3/4 cups	425 mL
Package of frozen puff pastry (14 oz., 397 g), thawed according to package directions (see Note)	1/2	1/2

Heat large greased frying pan on medium-high. Add chicken. Heat and stir for 2 to 3 minutes until browned.

Add vegetables. Cook for about 4 minutes, stirring often, until liquid is evaporated and vegetables are tender-crisp.

Add pasta sauce. Stir. Spread in ungreased 9 x 13 inch (22 x 33 cm) baking dish.

Roll out 1 square of pastry on lightly floured surface to 10 x 14 inch (25 x 35 cm) rectangle. Place on top of chicken mixture. Press pastry up side of dish. Cut several small slits in top to allow steam to escape. Bake in 400°F (205°C) oven for about 30 minutes until pastry is golden. Serves 6.

1 serving: 551 Calories; 34.8 g Total Fat (9.6 g Mono, 8.8 g Poly, 14.2 g Sat); 98 mg Cholesterol; 30 g Carbohydrate; 3 g Fibre; 31 g Protein; 519 mg Sodium

Note: Use both squares of puff pastry if you like a thicker crust.

Cranberry Pesto Chicken

This tangy chicken dish is simple to prepare and tastes fantastic.
Serve with Orange Basil Couscous, page 111.

Bone-in chicken thighs, skin removed	3 lbs.	1.4 kg
Whole cranberry sauce	1 cup	250 mL
Barbecue sauce	1/4 cup	60 mL
Basil pesto	1/4 cup	60 mL

Arrange chicken thighs in greased 9 x 13 inch (22 x 33 cm) baking dish. Sprinkle with salt and pepper.

Combine remaining 3 ingredients in medium bowl. Spoon onto chicken. Bake, covered, in 350°F (175°C) oven for 1 hour. Bake, uncovered, for another 25 to 30 minutes until chicken is no longer pink inside. Remove chicken to large serving platter. Skim any fat from surface of sauce. Spoon sauce onto chicken. Serves 6.

1 serving: 280 Calories; 9.9 g Total Fat (4 g Mono, 2.1 g Poly, 2.2 g Sat); 113 mg Cholesterol; 20 g Carbohydrate; 1 g Fibre; 26 g Protein; 105 mg Sodium

Pictured on page 108.

Ginger Apricot Chicken

People will think you've worked all day on this scrumptious grilled chicken dish.

Zesty Italian dressing	2/3 cup	150 mL
Finely grated, peeled gingerroot	1 tbsp.	15 mL
Boneless, skinless chicken breast halves	4	4
(4 – 6 oz., 113 – 170 g, each)		
Apricot jam	1/2 cup	125 mL

Combine dressing and ginger in large resealable freezer bag. Add chicken breast halves. Seal bag. Turn until coated. Marinate in refrigerator for at least 6 hours or overnight, turning occasionally. Drain, reserving 1/3 cup (75 mL) marinade in small saucepan. Discard any remaining marinade.

(continued on next page)

Add jam to reserved marinade. Stir. Heat on medium until boiling. Reduce heat to medium-low. Simmer, uncovered, for at least 5 minutes. Preheat gas barbecue to medium-low (see Note). Cook chicken on greased grill for about 8 minutes per side, turning occasionally and brushing with jam mixture, until no longer pink inside. Serves 4.

1 serving: *453 Calories; 23.9 g Total Fat (12.5 g Mono, 7.7 g Poly, 2.2 g Sat); 102 mg Cholesterol; 29 g Carbohydrate; trace Fibre; 32 g Protein; 506 mg Sodium*

Note: Chicken may be broiled in the oven. Place chicken breast halves on a greased broiler pan. Brush with marinade. Broil on the top rack for 8 minutes. Turn. Brush with marinade. Broil for another 8 to 10 minutes until no longer pink inside.

Polynesian Chicken

A few convenient ingredients, and you've got delicious sweet and sour-sauced chicken everyone will love! Use apricot jam instead of marmalade if you prefer.

Bone-in chicken thighs, skin removed	3 lbs.	1.4 kg
Thousand Island dressing	1 cup	250 mL
Orange marmalade	1 cup	250 mL
Envelope of onion soup mix	2 oz.	55 g

Arrange chicken thighs in greased 9 x 13 inch (22 x 33 cm) baking dish.

Combine remaining 3 ingredients in small bowl. Pour over chicken. Bake, covered, in 350°F (175°C) oven for about 1 1/2 hours, turning chicken halfway through cooking time, until no longer pink inside. Remove cover for last 15 minutes to thicken sauce if desired. Serves 6.

1 serving: *519 Calories; 23.4 g Total Fat (11.2 g Mono, 7 g Poly, 3.1 g Sat); 125 mg Cholesterol; 50 g Carbohydrate; 1 g Fibre; 28 g Protein; 1160 mg Sodium*

Pictured on page 35.

Cheesy Broccoli Chicken

*Cheese, broccoli and tender chicken quickly combine into
a good weeknight casserole. Try it over a baked potato.*

Ground chicken	1 lb.	454 g
Frozen chopped broccoli	3 cups	750 mL
Can of condensed broccoli and cheese soup	10 oz.	284 mL
Grated medium Cheddar cheese	1 1/2 cups	375 mL

Scramble-fry ground chicken in large greased frying pan on medium for about 10 minutes until no longer pink.

Add broccoli, soup and a sprinkle of salt and pepper. Stir well. Spread in greased 1 1/2 quart (1.5 L) casserole.

Sprinkle with cheese. Bake, uncovered, in 350°F (175°C) oven for about 40 minutes until sauce is bubbling around edges. Serves 4.

1 serving: 548 Calories; 39.1 g Total Fat (7.4 g Mono, 1.5 g Poly, 13.7 g Sat); 65 mg Cholesterol; 13 g Carbohydrate; 3 g Fibre; 38 g Protein; 954 mg Sodium

Turkey Cannelloni

*A great way to use up leftover turkey. Oven-ready pasta tubes and
a simple red pepper sauce make this dish quick and delicious.*

Finely chopped red pepper	1 cup	250 mL
Cans of condensed cream of mushroom soup (10 oz., 284 mL, each)	2	2
Chopped cooked turkey	2 1/2 cups	625 mL
Oven-ready cannelloni pasta shells	12	12

Heat medium greased frying pan on medium. Add red pepper. Cook for about 2 minutes, stirring occasionally, until tender-crisp.

(continued on next page)

Add soup. Stir well. Transfer 1/2 cup (125 mL) to medium bowl. Set aside remaining soup mixture in pan.

Add turkey and a sprinkle of pepper to soup mixture in bowl. Stir. Spoon into pasta shells. Arrange in greased 9 x 13 inch (22 x 33 cm) baking dish. Add 2 1/2 cups (625 mL) water and a sprinkle of pepper to soup mixture in pan. Stir well. Pour over shells. Bake, covered, in 350°F (175°C) oven for about 40 minutes until sauce is bubbling. Bake, uncovered, for another 20 to 30 minutes until pasta is tender and sauce is slightly thickened. Serves 4.

1 serving: 446 Calories; 14.9 g Total Fat (2.9 g Mono, 6.5 g Poly, 4.2 g Sat); 112 mg Cholesterol; 36 g Carbohydrate; 2 g Fibre; 40 g Protein; 1299 mg Sodium

Chicken Shake

The Cajun-spiced, crispy coating resembles fried chicken, without the frying! Increase the Cajun seasoning for extra kick.

Biscuit mix	1/2 cup	125 mL
Cajun seasoning	2 tsp.	10 mL
Poultry seasoning	1 1/2 tsp.	7 mL
Chicken drumsticks (4 – 6 oz., 113 – 170 g, each)	12	12

Combine first 3 ingredients in large resealable freezer bag.

Sprinkle drumsticks with water. Place in bag. Seal. Toss until coated. Arrange drumsticks on greased baking sheet with sides. Spray with cooking spray. Bake in 350°F (175°C) oven for about 1 hour, turning once or twice, until chicken is no longer pink inside and coating is crisp and golden. Serves 6.

1 serving: 349 Calories; 22.7 g Total Fat (8.7 g Mono, 5.3 g Poly, 6.1 g Sat); 119 mg Cholesterol; 8 g Carbohydrate; trace Fibre; 27 g Protein; 250 mg Sodium

Pictured on page 125.

Sweet Orange Chicken

Grilled chicken coated in a dark, sweet sauce.
This barbecue recipe is the perfect choice for dinner
on the deck. Easy to double for a larger group.

Zesty Italian dressing	3/4 cup	175 mL
Brown sugar, packed	1/4 cup	60 mL
Grated orange zest	2 1/2 tsp.	12 mL
Chicken drumsticks (4 – 6 oz., 113 – 170 g, each), skin removed	12	12

Combine first 3 ingredients in large resealable freezer bag. Add drumsticks. Seal bag. Turn until coated. Marinate in refrigerator for at least 6 hours or overnight, turning occasionally. Drain marinade into small saucepan. Heat on medium until boiling. Reduce heat to medium-low. Simmer, uncovered, for at least 5 minutes. Preheat gas barbecue to medium-low. Cook chicken on greased grill for about 30 minutes, turning frequently and brushing occasionally with marinade, until no longer pink inside. Serves 6.

1 serving: 391 Calories; 28.1 g Total Fat (14 g Mono, 8.8 g Poly, 3.2 g Sat); 115 mg Cholesterol; 11 g Carbohydrate; trace Fibre; 23 g Protein; 494 mg Sodium

 If a barbecue flare-up occurs, move the food to one side of the grill until flames die down. If you must, a light spritz from a water bottle can control small flames, but serious flare-ups should be doused with baking soda.

Olive Chicken Patties

Olive tapenade adds marvelous Mediterranean flavour
to grilled chicken patties. Tasty with any
relish or a tzatziki cucumber sauce.

Large egg	1	1
Crushed seasoned croutons	3/4 cup	175 mL
Black olive tapenade	1/3 cup	75 mL
Lean ground chicken	1 lb.	454 g

Combine first 3 ingredients in large bowl.

Add ground chicken. Mix well. Shape into four 5 inch (12.5 cm) patties. Preheat gas barbecue to medium (see Note). Cook patties on greased grill for about 7 minutes per side until fully cooked, and internal temperature of chicken reaches 175°F (80°C). Makes 4 patties.

1 patty: 286 Calories; 18.8 g Total Fat (1.8 g Mono, 0.4 g Poly, 0.9 g Sat); 54 mg Cholesterol; 6 g Carbohydrate; 1 g Fibre; 22 g Protein; 252 mg Sodium

Pictured on page 107.

Note: Patties may be broiled in the oven. Place patties on a greased broiler pan. Broil on the top rack for about 7 minutes per side until fully cooked, and internal temperature of chicken reaches 175°F (80°C).

Oven Ranch Fries

Mild ranch seasoning adds tang to tender potatoes. If you want bolder flavour, double the amount of bread crumbs and dressing mix. Serve with sour cream and bacon dip.

Medium unpeeled potatoes, each cut lengthwise into 8 wedges	4	4
Cooking oil	2 tbsp.	30 mL
Fine dry bread crumbs	2 tbsp.	30 mL
Envelope of ranch dressing mix	1 oz.	28 g

Put potato wedges into large bowl. Drizzle with cooking oil. Toss until coated.

Combine bread crumbs and dressing mix in large resealable freezer bag. Add potato wedges in several batches. Seal bag. Toss until coated. Arrange on greased baking sheet. Bake in 375°F (190°C) oven for 45 to 50 minutes until tender and golden. Serves 4.

1 serving: 222 Calories; 9.6 g Total Fat (5.5 g Mono, 2.9 g Poly, 0.8 g Sat); 1 mg Cholesterol; 31 g Carbohydrate; 3 g Fibre; 4 g Protein; 542 mg Sodium

Pictured on page 71.

Greek Beans

Bright green beans are wonderful combined with sweet onion and flavourful feta cheese. Ready in just minutes!

Fresh (or frozen) whole green beans, halved	4 cups	1 L
Garlic butter	2 tbsp.	30 mL
Thinly sliced red onion	1/2 cup	125 mL
Crumbled olive-and-herb-flavoured feta cheese	1/2 cup	125 mL

(continued on next page)

Cook green beans in boiling water in large saucepan for about 3 minutes until bright green. Drain. Set aside.

Melt butter in large frying pan on medium. Add onion. Cook for about 2 minutes, stirring often, until starting to soften. Add beans. Cook for another 3 to 4 minutes, stirring occasionally, until beans are tender-crisp.

Add cheese and a sprinkle of salt and pepper. Stir. Serves 4.

1 serving: 150 Calories; 10.4 g Total Fat (2.6 g Mono, 0.4 g Poly, 6.7 g Sat); 34 mg Cholesterol; 11 g Carbohydrate; 2 g Fibre; 5 g Protein; 296 mg Sodium

Pictured on page 89.

Sweet Potato Sticks

Deliciously seasoned sweet potatoes are good any time!

Fresh medium sweet potatoes (or yams), peeled	2	2
Olive oil	2 tbsp.	30 mL
Montreal chicken spice	2 tsp.	10 mL
Lemon pepper	1 tsp.	5 mL

Cut potatoes lengthwise into 1/2 inch (12 mm) slices. Cut slices lengthwise into 1/2 inch (12 mm) sticks. Put into large bowl. Drizzle with olive oil. Toss until coated.

Combine chicken spice and lemon pepper in large resealable freezer bag. Add potato sticks. Seal bag. Toss until coated. Arrange on greased baking sheet. Bake in 425°F (220°C) oven for 20 to 25 minutes until tender. Serves 4.

1 serving: 209 Calories; 7.3 g Total Fat (5.1 g Mono, 0.8 g Poly, 1 g Sat); 0 mg Cholesterol; 34 g Carbohydrate; 4 g Fibre; 2 g Protein; 463 mg Sodium

Pictured on page 125.

Pineapple Ginger Carrots

Slightly sweetened with a pineapple ginger glaze, these carrots are great paired with rice and baked ham or pork roast.

Hard margarine (or butter)	2 tbsp.	30 mL
Finely grated, peeled gingerroot	1/2 tsp.	2 mL
Bag of baby carrots, larger ones cut in half	1 lb.	454 g
Frozen concentrated pineapple juice	1/3 cup	75 mL

Melt margarine in large frying pan on medium. Add ginger. Heat and stir for about 1 minute until fragrant.

Add carrots and a sprinkle of salt and pepper. Stir until coated. Add concentrated pineapple juice. Stir. Cook, covered, for about 8 minutes until carrots are tender-crisp. Remove cover. Heat and stir for 1 to 2 minutes until liquid is evaporated and carrots are glazed. Serves 4.

1 serving: 146 Calories; 6 g Total Fat (3.8 g Mono, 0.7 g Poly, 1.2 g Sat); 0 mg Cholesterol; 23 g Carbohydrate; 3 g Fibre; 2 g Protein; 108 mg Sodium

Pictured on page 126.

Fruity Stuffing

Serve this baked bread-and-apple stuffing with pork or poultry dishes. Bake it inside a crown roast of pork for an impressive presentation.

Chopped onion	1 1/2 cups	375 mL
Can of apple pie filling	19 oz.	540 mL
Poultry seasoning (or dried sage)	1 tsp.	5 mL
Box of seasoned croutons	6 oz.	170 g

(continued on next page)

Heat large greased frying pan on medium. Add onion. Cook for 5 to 10 minutes, stirring often, until softened. Remove from heat.

Add pie filling. Break up larger pieces of apple with spoon. Add poultry seasoning and a sprinkle of salt and pepper. Stir.

Add croutons and 1/4 cup (60 mL) water. Mix well. Transfer to well-greased 2 quart (2 L) casserole. Bake, covered, in 350°F (175°C) oven for about 45 minutes until heated through and croutons are softened. Serves 6.

1 serving: 262 Calories; 6.9 g Total Fat (3.6 g Mono, 1.2 g Poly, 1.6 g Sat); 1 mg Cholesterol; 48 g Carbohydrate; 3 g Fibre; 4 g Protein; 396 mg Sodium

Wild Rice Medley

Filled with Mediterranean flavours, this double-duty side dish makes an appetizing stuffing for chicken, or a pork or turkey roll.

Package of long grain and wild rice mix (with seasoning packet)	**6 1/4 oz.**	**180 g**
Garlic butter	**3 tbsp.**	**50 mL**
Chopped onion	**1 cup**	**250 mL**
Sun-dried tomatoes in oil, drained and chopped	**1/2 cup**	**125 mL**

Combine rice with seasoning packet and 2 1/4 cups (550 mL) water in medium saucepan. Bring to a boil. Reduce heat to medium-low. Simmer, covered, for about 30 minutes until liquid is absorbed. Remove from heat. Let stand, covered, for 5 minutes. Fluff with a fork.

Melt butter in large frying pan on medium. Add onion and sun-dried tomato. Cook for 5 to 10 minutes, stirring often, until onion is softened. Add rice. Heat and stir for about 1 minute until heated through. Serves 4.

1 serving: 285 Calories; 11.5 g Total Fat (4 g Mono, 0.9 g Poly, 5.9 g Sat); 24 mg Cholesterol; 41 g Carbohydrate; 2 g Fibre; 6 g Protein; 596 mg Sodium

Pictured on page 126.

Grilled Dijon Polenta

*The mild corn flavour of this roasted side dish will fit
at any meal. Use more mustard for a bolder taste.*

Prepared chicken broth	4 cups	1 L
Yellow cornmeal	1 1/2 cups	375 mL
Grated Asiago cheese	1/4 cup	60 mL
Dijon mustard	3 tbsp.	50 mL

Combine broth and a sprinkle of salt and pepper in large saucepan. Bring
to a boil. Reduce heat to medium. Slowly add cornmeal, stirring constantly.
Heat and stir for about 10 minutes until mixture thickens and pulls away
from side of saucepan.

Add cheese and mustard. Stir. Line 9 x 9 inch (22 x 22 cm) pan with
greased foil. Spread cornmeal mixture in pan. Chill for about 1 hour until
firm. Invert onto cutting board. Cut into 4 squares. Cut squares in half
diagonally, for a total of 8 triangles. Brush with cooking oil. Preheat gas
barbecue to medium. Cook polenta on well-greased grill for about
6 minutes per side until grill marks appear and polenta is heated through.
Makes 8 triangles.

*1 triangle: 138 Calories; 2.5 g Total Fat (0.8 g Mono, 0.6 g Poly, 0.9 g Sat); 3 mg Cholesterol;
22 g Carbohydrate; 1 g Fibre; 6 g Protein; 505 mg Sodium*

Pictured on page 107.

1. Grilled Dijon Polenta, above.
2. Fruit Freeze, page 123
3. Tomato Bocconcini Salad, page 32
4. Olive Chicken Patties, page 101

Props courtesy of: Canhome Global
Cherison Enterprises Inc.
Pfaltzgraff Canada

Stuffin' Muffins

Serve these hot from the oven with any poultry dish.

Large oranges	2	2
Boxes of chicken stove-top stuffing mix (4 1/4 oz., 120 g, each)	2	2
Chopped pecans, toasted (see Tip, page 21)	1 cup	250 mL
Dried cranberries	1/4 cup	60 mL

Grate 1 tbsp. (15 mL) orange zest into medium saucepan. Squeeze oranges. Transfer juice to 4 cup (1 L) liquid measure. Add enough water to make 2 1/4 cups (550 mL). Add to zest.

Add seasoning packets from stuffing mixes. Stir. Bring to a boil. Add stuffing, pecans and cranberries. Stir. Remove from heat. Let stand for about 10 minutes until liquid is absorbed. Fluff with a fork. Spoon into 12 greased muffin cups. Bake in 350°F (175°C) oven for about 12 minutes until heated through and starting to brown. Makes 12 muffins.

1 muffin: 159 Calories; 7.7 g Total Fat (4.7 g Mono, 1.9 g Poly, 0.7 g Sat); 0 mg Cholesterol; 20 g Carbohydrate; 1 g Fibre; 3 g Protein; 318 mg Sodium

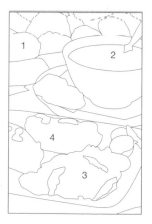

1 Parmesan Olive Biscuits, page 30
2. Pumpkin Soup, page 47
3. Orange Basil Couscous, page 111
4. Cranberry Pesto Chicken, page 96

Props courtesy of: Cherison Enterprises Inc.
                    Danesco Inc.
                    Out of the Fire Studio

Saucy Polenta Alfredo

Soft polenta smothered in a rich sauce, accented nicely
with smoky ham. A comforting, cold-weather dish.

Sliced fresh white mushrooms	1 cup	250 mL
Black Forest ham slices, cut into thin strips	6 oz.	170 g
Alfredo pasta sauce	1 3/4 cups	425 mL
Polenta roll, cut into 1/2 inch (12 mm) slices	1 1/8 lbs.	510 g

Heat large greased frying pan on medium-high. Add mushrooms. Heat and stir for 1 minute. Reduce heat to medium-low. Add ham and pasta sauce. Stir. Bring to a boil, stirring occasionally.

Place polenta slices on top of sauce. Boil gently, covered, for about 10 minutes, turning slices over after 5 minutes, until polenta is heated through. Serves 4.

1 serving: 444 Calories; 32.2 g Total Fat (10.3 g Mono, 1.8 g Poly, 18.2 g Sat); 97 mg Cholesterol; 18 g Carbohydrate; 1 g Fibre; 21 g Protein; 1097 mg Sodium

Spinach And Lentil Sauté

A wholesome lentil side dish. Outstanding flavour,
and an attractive addition to any meal.

Garlic butter	1/4 cup	60 mL
Chopped onion	1/2 cup	125 mL
Box of frozen chopped spinach, thawed and squeezed dry	10 oz.	300 g
Can of lentils, rinsed and drained	19 oz.	540 mL

Melt butter in large frying pan on medium-high. Add onion. Cook for about 3 minutes, stirring often, until starting to brown.

Add spinach, lentils and a sprinkle of salt and pepper. Heat and stir for about 2 minutes until heated through. Serves 4.

1 serving: 214 Calories; 12.8 g Total Fat (3.6 g Mono, 0.7 g Poly, 7.7 g Sat); 33 mg Cholesterol; 19 g Carbohydrate; 5 g Fibre; 9 g Protein; 341 mg Sodium

Orange Basil Couscous

Sweet oranges and fragrant basil make delicate couscous an interesting side for pork chops or grilled chicken breasts.

Medium oranges	2	2
Package of couscous with fruit and nuts	7 oz.	198 g
Spicy olive oil with herbs	2 tsp.	10 mL
Chopped fresh basil	1 tbsp.	15 mL

Grate 1/2 tsp. (2 mL) orange zest into medium bowl. Peel and segment oranges (see Tip, page 33). Cut segments into thirds. Add to zest. Stir. Set aside.

Measure 2 cups (500 mL) water into large saucepan. Bring to a boil. Add couscous and olive oil. Stir. Remove from heat. Let stand, covered, for 5 minutes. Fluff with a fork.

Add orange mixture and basil. Stir. Serves 4.

1 serving: 256 Calories; 4.2 g Total Fat (2.1 g Mono, 1.2 g Poly, 0.5 g Sat); 0 mg Cholesterol; 47 g Carbohydrate; 3 g Fibre; 8 g Protein; 470 mg Sodium

Pictured on page 108.

Paré Pointer

The movie had a happy ending. We were all glad it was over.

Salsa Rice

Jazz up long grain rice for a spicy side dish. Cilantro adds a tasty touch!

Long grain white rice	1 cup	250 mL
Can of condensed chicken broth with garlic and herbs	10 oz.	284 mL
Medium salsa	1/2 cup	125 mL
Chopped fresh cilantro or parsley	1 tbsp.	15 mL

Heat medium well-greased saucepan on medium. Add rice. Heat and stir for about 8 minutes until starting to brown.

Add broth, salsa and 1/2 cup (125 mL) water. Stir. Bring to a boil. Reduce heat to medium-low. Simmer, covered, for 15 to 20 minutes, without stirring, until liquid is absorbed and rice is tender.

Sprinkle with cilantro. Fluff with a fork until combined. Serves 4.

1 serving: 122 Calories; 3.3 g Total Fat (1.8 g Mono, 0.9 g Poly, 0.5 g Sat); 1 mg Cholesterol; 18 g Carbohydrate; 1 g Fibre; 5 g Protein; 562 mg Sodium

Creamed Spinach Casserole

This enticing dish can also be served as a spread for crackers. Even the kids will want to eat their spinach!

Boxes of frozen chopped spinach (10 oz., 300 g, each), thawed and squeezed dry	2	2
Tub of vegetable light spreadable cream cheese	8 oz.	250 g
Crushed seasoned croutons	1 cup	250 mL
Hard margarine (or butter), melted	2 tbsp.	30 mL

(continued on next page)

Combine spinach and cream cheese in medium bowl. Spread in greased 1 quart (1 L) casserole.

Combine crushed croutons and margarine in small bowl. Sprinkle over spinach mixture. Bake, uncovered, in 350°F (175°C) oven for about 40 minutes until crumbs are golden. Serves 6.

1 serving: 188 Calories; 14.3 g Total Fat (6.2 g Mono, 1.2 g Poly, 5.9 g Sat); 26 mg Cholesterol; 9 g Carbohydrate; 3 g Fibre; 7 g Protein; 485 mg Sodium

Tomato Risotto

This creamy risotto is sublime with just a hint of garlic.
Serve with Italian sausage or grilled herbed chicken breasts.

Vegetable juice	3 cups	750 mL
Garlic butter	1/4 cup	60 mL
Arborio rice	1 1/2 cups	375 mL
Grated Parmesan cheese	3/4 cup	175 mL

Combine juice and 3 cups (750 mL) water in medium saucepan. Bring to a boil. Reduce heat to low. Cover.

Heat butter in large pot or Dutch oven on medium until melted. Add rice. Stir until coated. Add 1 cup (250 mL) juice mixture, stirring constantly until liquid is absorbed. Repeat with remaining juice mixture, 1 cup (250 mL) at a time, until all liquid is absorbed and rice is tender.

Add Parmesan cheese. Stir. Serves 6.

1 serving: 346 Calories; 12.5 g Total Fat (3.6 g Mono, 0.5 g Poly, 7.7 g Sat); 32 mg Cholesterol; 48 g Carbohydrate; 1 g Fibre; 10 g Protein; 797 mg Sodium

Paré Pointer

She ran outside and called, "Am I too late for the garbage?"
They replied, "No, just jump in."

Tangy Roasted Mushrooms

Try these mushrooms when you barbecue fish, chicken or pork.

Medium orange	1	1
Balsamic vinegar	1/4 cup	60 mL
Italian seasoning	1/2 tsp.	2 mL
Portobello mushrooms	6	6

Grate 1 tsp. (5 mL) orange zest into small bowl. Squeeze orange. Add juice to zest. Add vinegar and seasoning. Stir.

Discard mushroom stems. Cut mushroom caps into quarters. Arrange, gill-side up, in ungreased 9 x 13 inch (22 x 33 cm) baking dish. Pour orange juice mixture over mushrooms. Bake, uncovered, in 425°F (220°C) oven for 20 minutes. Turn mushrooms over. Bake for another 5 minutes until liquid is absorbed and mushrooms are browned. Sprinkle with salt and pepper. Serves 4.

1 serving: 68 Calories; 1 g Total Fat (0 g Mono, 0.4 g Poly, 0.1 g Sat); 0 mg Cholesterol; 14 g Carbohydrate; 3 g Fibre; 5 g Protein; 58 mg Sodium

Fragrant Rice

A wonderful aroma wafts from this sweetened rice.
Sure to make mouths water.

Large orange	1	1
Converted white rice	1 1/2 cups	375 mL
Chai tea concentrate	1 cup	250 mL
Dark raisins	1/4 cup	60 mL

Grate 2 tsp. (10 mL) orange zest into small bowl. Set aside. Squeeze orange. Transfer juice to 2 cup (500 mL) liquid measure. Add enough water to make 2 cups (500 mL). Pour into medium saucepan.

(continued on next page)

Add rice, tea concentrate and a generous sprinkle of salt. Stir. Bring to a boil. Reduce heat to medium-low. Simmer, covered, for about 18 minutes until liquid is absorbed and rice is tender.

Add orange zest, raisins and a sprinkle of salt and pepper. Stir. Serves 4.

1 serving: 313 Calories; 0.5 g Total Fat (0.1 g Mono, 0.1 g Poly, 0.1 g Sat); 0 mg Cholesterol; 70 g Carbohydrate; 1 g Fibre; 5 g Protein; 6 mg Sodium

Sweet Onion Squash

*Buttery garlic and Parmesan cheese lend
a Mediterranean flair to this delicious side dish.*

Butternut squash, peeled and cubed	1 1/2 lbs.	680 g
Garlic butter	2 tbsp.	30 mL
Chopped onion	1 cup	250 mL
Grated Parmesan cheese	1/4 cup	60 mL

Cook squash in boiling water in large saucepan until tender. Drain. Mash. Cover to keep warm.

Melt butter in medium frying pan on medium. Add onion. Cook for 5 to 10 minutes, stirring often, until onion is softened and starting to brown. Add to squash. Stir well.

Add Parmesan cheese. Stir until cheese is melted. Serves 4.

1 serving: 162 Calories; 8.1 g Total Fat (2.3 g Mono, 0.4 g Poly, 4.9 g Sat); 21 mg Cholesterol; 21 g Carbohydrate; 3 g Fibre; 5 g Protein; 190 mg Sodium

Paré Pointer

*The least expensive plastic surgery is simply cutting up
your credit cards.*

Roasted Onions

Slow roasting gives onions a sweet, mellow flavour. Great with roast beef.

Balsamic vinegar	3 tbsp.	50 mL
Olive oil	2 tbsp.	30 mL
Italian seasoning	1/2 tsp.	2 mL
Sweet medium onions (such as Vidalia), each cut into 12 wedges	3	3

Combine first 3 ingredients and a sprinkle of salt and pepper in large bowl.

Add onion. Toss until coated. Spread on greased baking sheet with sides. Bake in 375°F (190°C) oven for about 30 minutes, stirring occasionally, until softened and browned. Serves 10.

1 serving: 47 Calories; 3.7 g Total Fat (2.6 g Mono, 0.5 g Poly, 0.4 g Sat); 0 mg Cholesterol; 3 g Carbohydrate; 1 g Fibre; 0 g Protein; 21 mg Sodium

Ginger Curry Rice

Vibrant sticky rice with a pleasant, lingering heat.

Finely grated, peeled gingerroot (or 1/2 tsp., 2 mL, ground ginger)	2 tsp.	10 mL
Curry powder	1 tsp.	5 mL
Long grain white rice	1 cup	250 mL
Mango chutney, larger pieces cut smaller	1/4 cup	60 mL

Heat medium well-greased saucepan on medium. Add ginger and curry powder. Heat and stir for about 1 minute until fragrant.

Add rice and a sprinkle of salt and pepper. Heat and stir on medium for about 2 minutes until rice is golden. Add 2 cups (500 mL) water. Heat and stir for about 5 minutes until boiling. Reduce heat to medium-low. Simmer, covered, for about 15 minutes until liquid is absorbed and rice is tender.

Add chutney. Stir. Serves 4.

1 serving: 217 Calories; 2.7 g Total Fat (1.5 g Mono, 0.8 g Poly, 0.3 g Sat); 0 mg Cholesterol; 44 g Carbohydrate; 1 g Fibre; 4 g Protein; 3 mg Sodium

Texas-Style Caviar

Everything's bigger in Texas! These zesty black beans look like "giant caviar." Use twice as much cilantro for added fresh flavour. A spicy side for barbecued ribs or chicken.

Can of black beans, rinsed and drained	19 oz.	540 mL
Chipotle chili pepper in adobo sauce, finely chopped (see Note)	1	1
Zesty Italian dressing	1/3 cup	75 mL
Chopped fresh cilantro or parsley	2 tbsp.	30 mL

Combine all 4 ingredients in medium bowl. Cover. Chill for at least 1 hour to blend flavours. Makes about 2 cups (500 mL).

2 tbsp. (30 mL): 53 Calories; 3.5 g Total Fat (1.9 g Mono, 1.2 g Poly, 0.3 g Sat); 3 mg Cholesterol; 4 g Carbohydrate; 1 g Fibre, 1 g Protein; 167 mg Sodium

Note: Store leftover chipotle chili peppers and sauce in a clean jar in the refrigerator for several months.

Glazed Mushrooms

Shiny, teriyaki-glazed mushrooms with a subtle orange accent. There's lots of tasty sauce to drizzle over rice and grilled chicken.

Thick teriyaki basting sauce	1/4 cup	60 mL
Rice vinegar	1 tbsp.	15 mL
Frozen concentrated orange juice, thawed	1 tbsp.	15 mL
Small fresh whole white mushrooms	1 lb.	454 g

Combine first 3 ingredients in small bowl. Set aside.

Heat large greased frying pan on medium. Add mushrooms. Heat and stir for about 10 minutes until starting to brown. Add teriyaki mixture. Heat and stir for about 2 minutes until mushrooms are glazed. Serves 4.

1 serving: 73 Calories; 2.8 g Total Fat (1.4 g Mono, 0.9 g Poly, 0.2 g Sat); 0 mg Cholesterol; 10 g Carbohydrate; 2 g Fibre; 4 g Protein; 740 mg Sodium

Squash-ghetti And Sauce

Once you cook spaghetti squash, you'll discover how it got its name.
The flesh separates into thin, slightly firm strands. Smothered in zesty tomato
sauce and Parmesan cheese, it's certain to become a favourite!

Spaghetti squash	4 3/4 lbs.	2.2 kg
Medium unpeeled zucchini, quartered lengthwise and cut into 1/2 inch (12 mm) pieces	1	1
Tomato pasta sauce with mushrooms and green pepper	2 3/4 cups	675 mL
Grated Parmesan cheese	1/2 cup	125 mL

Cut squash in half lengthwise. Discard seeds. Place, cut-side down, in microwave-safe 3 quart (3 L) casserole. Cover. Microwave on high (100%) for 20 to 30 minutes until flesh is tender and can be shredded into strands with a fork. Let stand, covered, for about 20 minutes until cool enough to handle. Shred flesh into large serving bowl. Cover to keep warm.

Heat medium greased saucepan on medium. Add zucchini. Cook for about 5 minutes, stirring occasionally, until starting to soften.

Add pasta sauce. Stir. Bring to a boil. Pour over squash. Toss gently until coated.

Sprinkle with Parmesan cheese. Serves 6.

1 serving: 267 Calories; 10.7 g Total Fat (4.3 g Mono, 2.5 g Poly, 2.9 g Sat); 7 mg Cholesterol; 38 g Carbohydrate; 5 g Fibre; 8 g Protein; 807 mg Sodium

Colourful Couscous

This simple-to-make dish is great paired with Tomato Bocconcini Salad,
page 32, when you're serving pork chops or grilled chicken.

Vegetable juice	2 cups	500 mL
Packages of couscous with mushrooms (7 oz., 198 g, each)	2	2
Fresh stir-fry vegetable mix	4 cups	1 L
Sun-dried tomato pesto	3 tbsp.	50 mL

(continued on next page)

Combine juice and 2 1/4 cups (550 mL) water in large saucepan. Reserve 1/2 cup (125 mL). Bring juice mixture in pan to a boil.

Add couscous. Stir. Remove from heat. Let stand, covered, for 5 minutes. Fluff with a fork.

Heat greased wok or large frying pan on medium-high. Add vegetables. Stir-fry for 3 minutes.

Add reserved juice mixture and pesto. Stir-fry for another 2 to 3 minutes until vegetables are coated and liquid is evaporated. Add couscous. Stir-fry for about 1 minute until heated through. Serves 6.

1 serving: 306 Calories; 2.8 g Total Fat (1.4 g Mono, 0.8 g Poly, 0.3 g Sat); trace Cholesterol; 60 g Carbohydrate; 4 g Fibre; 11 g Protein; 570 mg Sodium

Pictured on page 90.

Orange Squash Bowls

Sweet, orange couscous sits pretty in squash shells.
A delicious dish that's on the table in about 30 minutes.

Medium acorn squash	2	2
Orange juice	2 1/2 cups	625 mL
Package of couscous with mushrooms	7 oz.	198 g
Chopped dried apricot	1/2 cup	125 mL

Cut both squash in half lengthwise. Discard seeds. Place 2 halves, cut-side down, in microwave-safe 2 quart (2 L) casserole. Pour 1/4 cup (60 mL) water into casserole. Cover. Microwave on high (100%) for about 10 minutes until squash is tender. Repeat with remaining halves. Scoop about 3 tbsp. (50 mL) flesh from each half into small bowl. Set aside. Place shells, cut-side up, on large oven-safe serving platter. Place in 300°F (150°C) oven to keep warm.

Measure orange juice into medium saucepan. Bring to a boil. Add couscous. Stir. Remove from heat. Let stand, covered, for 5 minutes. Fluff with a fork.

Heat large greased frying pan on medium. Add squash flesh, couscous and apricot. Sprinkle with salt and pepper. Heat and stir for about 5 minutes until starting to brown. Spoon into squash shells. Serves 4.

1 serving: 421 Calories; 4.5 g Total Fat (2.2 g Mono, 1.4 g Poly, 0.4 g Sat); 0 mg Cholesterol; 89 g Carbohydrate; 7 g Fibre; 10 g Protein; 177 mg Sodium

Chocolate Hazelnut Angel

*Sweet and crunchy, the chocolate-hazelnut glaze on
this light-textured angel food cake is heavenly!*

Box of angel food cake mix	16 oz.	450 g
Hazelnut liqueur, divided	1/3 cup	75 mL
Flaked hazelnuts (filberts), toasted (see Tip, page 21), divided	2/3 cup	150 mL
Chocolate hazelnut spread	1/2 cup	125 mL

Prepare cake mix according to package directions, adding 2 tbsp. (30 mL) liqueur to liquid ingredients.

Reserve 2 tbsp. (30 mL) hazelnuts in small cup. Fold remaining hazelnuts into batter. Spread in ungreased 10 inch (25 cm) angel food tube pan. Bake in 325°F (160°C) oven for about 55 minutes until wooden pick inserted in centre of cake comes out clean. Invert cake in pan onto glass bottle for 2 to 3 hours until cooled completely. Turn upright. Run knife around inside edge of pan to loosen cake. Remove bottom of pan with cake. Run knife around tube and bottom of pan to loosen. Invert cake onto large serving plate.

Combine chocolate spread and remaining liqueur in small saucepan. Heat and stir on low for about 6 minutes until smooth. Cool slightly. Drizzle over cake. Sprinkle with reserved hazelnuts. Chill for 30 minutes. Cuts into 12 wedges (see Tip, below).

*1 wedge: 275 Calories; 10.2 g Total Fat (6.1 g Mono, 2.1 g Poly, 1.5 g Sat); 0 mg Cholesterol;
38 g Carbohydrate; 1 g Fibre; 7 g Protein; 330 mg Sodium*

 tip   The best way to cut an angel food cake is to use a serrated knife and
a gentle sawing motion. Wipe the knife clean after each cut.

Lemon Coconut Angel

An attractive, three-tiered angel food cake filled
with sweet lemon and coconut. Lovely!

Angel food cake	1	1
Can of lemon pie filling, divided	19 oz.	540 mL
Medium unsweetened coconut, toasted (see Tip, page 21)	1 cup	250 mL
Frozen whipped topping, thawed	2 cups	500 mL

Cut cake horizontally into 3 layers. Place largest, bottom layer, cut-side up, on large serving plate.

Reserve 1/2 cup (125 mL) lemon pie filling in small bowl. Put remaining pie filling into separate small bowl. Add 1/2 cup (125 mL) coconut. Stir. Spread 1/2 of coconut mixture on bottom cake layer. Place centre cake layer on top of coconut mixture. Spread with remaining coconut mixture. Cover with smallest, top cake layer, cut-side down.

Add whipped topping to reserved pie filling. Stir. Spread on top and side of cake. Sprinkle with remaining coconut. Chill for about 1 hour until filling is firm. Cuts into 12 wedges (see Tip, page 120).

1 wedge: 272 Calories; 8.7 g Total Fat (0.4 g Mono, 0.2 g Poly, 7.4 g Sat); 0 mg Cholesterol; 47 g Carbohydrate; 1 g Fibre; 4 g Protein; 281 mg Sodium

Pictured on page 35.

Paré Pointer

Bakers make good baseball pitchers because they know their batter.

Chai Ice Cream

Pleasant, mild chai spices add delicate flavour to this light, icy dessert.

Egg yolks (large)	6	6
Granulated sugar	1/2 cup	125 mL
Chai tea concentrate	1/2 cup	125 mL
Half-and-half cream	4 cups	1 L

Beat egg yolks and sugar in large bowl for about 3 minutes until thick and pale. Add tea concentrate. Stir. Set aside.

Heat cream in large heavy saucepan on medium for about 10 minutes until very hot and bubbles appear around edge of saucepan. Slowly add tea mixture, stirring constantly. Heat and stir for about 8 minutes until slightly thickened and mixture coats back of metal spoon. Transfer to large heatproof bowl. Let stand for 30 minutes. Chill, uncovered, for at least 3 hours until very cold. Pour into ice cream maker (see Note). Follow manufacturer's instructions. Makes about 6 cups (1.5 L).

1 cup (250 mL): 329 Calories; 22.2 g Total Fat (6.9 g Mono, 1.3 g Poly, 12.2 g Sat); 269 mg Cholesterol; 25 g Carbohydrate; 0 g Fibre; 8 g Protein; 78 mg Sodium

Note: If you don't have an ice cream maker, spread the mixture in a 9 x 9 inch (22 x 22 cm) pan. Freeze, stirring every hour for 4 hours.

Paré Pointer

The easiest way to see flying saucers is to pinch a waitress.

Fruit Freeze

You'll love the smooth fruit flavour of this refreshing dessert.

Cans of fruit cocktail (14 oz., 398 mL, each), drained and juice reserved	2	2
Box of tropical-flavoured jelly powder (gelatin)	3 oz.	85 g
Vanilla yogurt	1 1/2 cups	375 mL
Egg white (large)	1	1

Measure 1/2 cup (125 mL) reserved juice into small saucepan. Bring to a boil. Remove from heat.

Add jelly powder. Stir until dissolved. Add remaining juice and fruit cocktail. Stir. Add yogurt. Stir well. Process in 2 batches in blender or food processor until smooth. Transfer to medium bowl. Set aside.

Beat egg white in small bowl until stiff peaks form. Gently fold in 1 cup (250 mL) fruit mixture. Fold egg white mixture into remaining fruit mixture in medium bowl. Transfer to 9 x 9 inch (22 x 22 cm) baking dish. Freeze, covered, for about 4 hours until gelled and ice crystals form. Scrape into large bowl. Beat on high until slushy. Pour into large airtight container. Freeze for at least 4 hours until firm. Let stand at room temperature for 15 minutes before serving. Makes about 6 cups (1.5 L).

1 cup (250 mL): 180 Calories; 1.2 g Total Fat (0.3 g Mono, 0 g Poly, 0.8 g Sat); 3 mg Cholesterol; 39 g Carbohydrate; 2 g Fibre; 5 g Protein; 88 mg Sodium

Pictured on page 107.

Paré Pointer

A football coach is desired, hired, wired, admired, tired, mired—then fired.

Tangy Rice Parfaits

Gorgeous raspberries on top of rice pudding and granola make this a showy dessert. Use vanilla bean yogurt for strongest vanilla flavour.

White basmati rice	3/4 cup	175 mL
Hazelnut and honey granola	1 cup	250 mL
Vanilla yogurt	1 cup	250 mL
Fresh raspberries	2 cups	500 mL

Measure 1 1/2 cups (375 mL) water into medium saucepan. Bring to a boil. Add rice and a sprinkle of salt. Stir. Reduce heat to medium-low. Simmer, covered, for about 15 minutes until water is absorbed. Remove from heat. Let stand, covered, for 5 minutes. Fluff with a fork. Cool.

Put granola into 4 parfait or medium glasses.

Add yogurt to rice. Stir. Spoon on top of granola.

Top with raspberries. Serves 4.

1 serving: 349 Calories; 5.9 g Total Fat (0.5 g Mono, 0.3 g Poly, 0.9 g Sat); 3 mg Cholesterol; 67 g Carbohydrate; 6 g Fibre; 9 g Protein; 86 mg Sodium

Pictured on front cover.

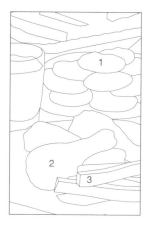

1. Chocolate Crunch Cookies, page 132
2. Chicken Shake, page 99
3. Sweet Potato Sticks, page 103

Props courtesy of: Cherison Enterprises Inc.

Desserts & Snacks

Ooey Gooey Bars

These bars go above and beyond the call of duty to satisfy a sweet tooth!
Macadamia nuts and scrumptious caramel top a chocolate chip cookie base.

Tubes of refrigerator chocolate chip cookie dough (18 oz., 510 g, each)	2	2
Package of caramel apple wraps	6 1/2 oz.	184 g
Coarsely chopped raw macadamia nuts	3/4 cup	175 mL
Skor (or Heath) bars (1 1/2 oz., 39 g, each), chopped	3	3

Let cookie dough stand at room temperature for about 15 minutes until starting to soften. Press into ungreased 9 × 13 inch (22 × 33 cm) pan. Bake in 375°F (190°C) oven for about 20 minutes until wooden pick inserted in centre comes out clean.

Arrange caramel wraps on top of cookie in pan to cover. Sprinkle with nuts and Skor pieces. Bake for another 5 minutes until Skor pieces and caramel are melted. Let stand on wire rack for 1 hour. Cuts into 32 bars.

1 bar: 206 Calories; 10.7 g Total Fat (5.2 g Mono, 0.7 g Poly, 3 g Sat); 10 mg Cholesterol; 26 g Carbohydrate; trace Fibre; 2 g Protein; 89 mg Sodium

Pictured on page 126.

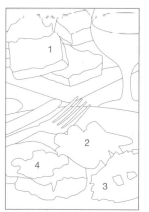

1. Ooey Gooey Bars, above
2. Pineapple Ginger Carrots, page 104
3. Wild Rice Medley, page 105
4. Glazed Pork Roast, page 84

Props courtesy of: Casa Bugatti
Danesco Inc.

VIP Cookies

Dark chocolate coats a peanut butter sandwich cookie. Sweet and addictive! Treat some very important person to a gift of cookies.

Smooth peanut butter	1/2 cup	125 mL
Vanilla wafers	48	48
Semi-sweet chocolate baking squares (1 oz., 28 g, each), chopped	8	8
Hard margarine (or butter)	1 tbsp.	15 mL

Spread peanut butter on bottom of 24 wafers. Cover with remaining wafers. Chill for about 1 hour until peanut butter is firm.

Heat chocolate and margarine in small heavy saucepan on lowest heat, stirring often, until chocolate is almost melted. Do not overheat. Remove from heat. Stir until smooth. Transfer to heatproof 1 cup (250 mL) liquid measure set in bowl of hot water. Hot water will prevent chocolate from hardening. Dip cookies into chocolate mixture until coated, allowing excess to drip back into liquid measure. Place on waxed paper-lined cookie sheet. Let stand until set. Drizzle any remaining chocolate in decorative pattern over cookies. Makes 2 dozen (24) cookies.

1 cookie: 118 Calories; 7.4 g Total Fat (3.1 g Mono, 1.2 g Poly, 2.6 g Sat); 5 mg Cholesterol; 13 g Carbohydrate; 1 g Fibre; 2 g Protein; 58 mg Sodium

Pictured on page 143.

Paré Pointer

Garage sales offer a good service. They distribute all their junk to lots of other garages.

Five-Spice Nut Crunch

A crunchy snack. These slightly sweet pecans are made for sharing with friends. Easy to double for a party.

Egg white (large)	1	1
Brown sugar, packed	1/3 cup	75 mL
Chinese five-spice powder	2 tsp.	10 mL
Pecan halves	3 cups	750 mL

Beat egg white in large bowl until frothy. Add brown sugar and five-spice powder. Stir well.

Add pecans. Stir until coated. Spread on parchment paper-lined baking sheet with sides. Bake in 350°F (175°C) oven for about 15 minutes, stirring occasionally, until golden and dry. Makes about 3 cups (750 mL).

1/4 cup (60 mL): 218 Calories; 19.5 g Total Fat (12.1 g Mono, 4.8 g Poly, 1.6 g Sat); 0 mg Cholesterol; 12 g Carbohydrate; 2 g Fibre; 3 g Protein; 8 mg Sodium

Pictured on page 17.

Blondie Brownies

Crunchy nuts and caramel flavour in a cake-like brownie. A not-too-sweet treat that's ready in a jiffy!

Biscuit mix	2 cups	500 mL
Brown sugar, packed	1 1/2 cups	375 mL
Large eggs	3	3
Chopped pecans	1 cup	250 mL

Beat first 3 ingredients in large bowl for about 3 minutes until smooth.

Add pecans. Stir. Spread in greased 9 x 9 inch (22 x 22 cm) pan. Bake in 350°F (175°C) oven for about 30 minutes until wooden pick inserted in centre comes out clean. Let stand on wire rack for 10 minutes. Cuts into 36 squares.

1 square: 98 Calories; 3.9 g Total Fat (2 g Mono, 1.1 g Poly, 0.6 g Sat); 18 mg Cholesterol; 15 g Carbohydrate; trace Fibre; 1 g Protein; 105 mg Sodium

Pictured on page 143.

Grab-And-Go Squares

A sweet, gooey blend of crunchy cereal and chewy dried fruit. Wrap individual squares tightly with plastic wrap, and they're ready to go! Are you?

Raisin bran cereal, coarsely crushed	6 cups	1.5 L
Chopped dried apricot	1/2 cup	125 mL
Hard margarine (or butter)	1/4 cup	60 mL
Package of miniature marshmallows	9 oz.	250 g

Combine cereal and apricot in extra-large bowl.

Melt margarine in large saucepan on medium. Add marshmallows. Heat and stir until smooth. Pour over cereal mixture. Stir until coated. Press in greased 9 × 13 inch (22 × 33 cm) pan. Chill until firm. Cuts into 15 squares.

1 square: 166 Calories; 3.6 g Total Fat (2.1 g Mono, 0.3 g Poly, 0.7 g Sat); 0 mg Cholesterol; 35 g Carbohydrate; 3 g Fibre; 2 g Protein; 186 mg Sodium

Pictured on page 144.

Strawberry Margarita Pie

This creamy strawberry filling tastes just like a strawberry margarita.

Box of strawberry-flavoured jelly powder (gelatin)	3 oz.	85 g
Medium limes	2	2
Frozen whipped topping, thawed	2 cups	500 mL
Chocolate crumb crust (9 inch, 22 cm, diameter)	1	1

Measure 3/4 cup (175 mL) boiling water into large heatproof bowl. Add jelly powder. Stir until dissolved. Grate 1 tsp. (5 mL) lime zest into small bowl. Squeeze lime juice. Add water, if needed, to make 1/2 cup (125 mL). Stir. Add to jelly mixture. Stir. Chill for at least 45 minutes, stirring occasionally, until very thick and starting to set. Beat for about 3 minutes until fluffy.

Fold in whipped topping until just combined. Spread in crumb crust. Chill for at least 2 hours until set. Cuts into 8 wedges.

1 wedge: 249 Calories; 13.7 g Total Fat (4.4 g Mono, 2.3 g Poly, 6.2 g Sat); 0 mg Cholesterol; 31 g Carbohydrate; trace Fibre; 3 g Protein; 220 mg Sodium

Pictured on page 143.

Desserts & Snacks

Hit-The-Trail Bars

Nutty, toasted-oat granola bars are a great snack. Wrap individual bars tightly with plastic wrap so they're ready to hit the trail when you are!

Quick-cooking rolled oats	4 cups	1 L
Coarsely chopped whole (or sliced) natural almonds	2 cups	500 mL
Can of sweetened condensed milk	11 oz.	300 mL
Hard margarine (or butter), melted	1/2 cup	125 mL

Combine rolled oats and almonds in large bowl.

Add condensed milk and margarine. Mix well. Spread in well-greased 10 × 15 inch (25 × 38 cm) jelly roll pan. Bake in 325°F (160°C) oven for about 25 minutes until golden. Let stand on wire rack for 5 to 10 minutes until slightly cooled. Cut while still warm into 16 bars.

1 bar: 333 Calories; 18.9 g Total Fat (10.9 g Mono, 3.2 g Poly, 3.7 g Sat); 8 mg Cholesterol; 34 g Carbohydrate; 4 g Fibre; 9 g Protein; 104 mg Sodium

Pictured on page 144.

Frozen Yogurt Tarts

Keep a supply of these creamy berry tarts in your freezer for a quick treat when company drops by.

Frozen mini tart shells, thawed	24	24
Container of blueberry yogurt	6 oz.	175 g
Block of cream cheese, softened	4 oz.	125 g
Blueberry jam	1/2 cup	125 mL

Place tart shells on baking sheet. Bake in 375°F (190°C) oven for 10 to 15 minutes until golden. Cool.

Beat remaining 3 ingredients in small bowl until smooth. Spoon into tart shells. Freeze for about 2 hours until firm. Makes 24 tarts.

1 tart: 91 Calories; 5 g Total Fat (2 g Mono, 0.5 g Poly, 2.2 g Sat); 6 mg Cholesterol; 11 g Carbohydrate; trace Fibre; 1 g Protein; 82 mg Sodium

Snap Brownies

Ready in a snap! These moist treats are just the ticket
when you want something sweet.

Unsweetened chocolate baking squares (1 oz., 28 g, each), chopped	3	3
Can of sweetened condensed milk	11 oz.	300 mL
Finely crushed vanilla wafers (about 48 wafers)	1 2/3 cups	400 mL
Chopped walnuts	1/2 cup	125 mL

Heat chocolate in large heavy saucepan on lowest heat, stirring often, until almost melted. Do not overheat. Remove from heat. Stir until smooth.

Add condensed milk. Stir. Add wafer crumbs and walnuts. Mix well. Spread in greased 8 × 8 inch (20 × 20 cm) pan. Bake in 300°F (150°C) oven for about 30 minutes until wooden pick inserted in centre comes out moist but not wet with batter. Do not overbake. Cool. Cuts into 25 squares.

1 square: 117 Calories; 5.9 g Total Fat (1.8 g Mono, 1.4 g Poly, 2.3 g Sat); 10 mg Cholesterol; 15 g Carbohydrate; 1 g Fibre; 3 g Protein; 44 mg Sodium

Pictured on page 143.

Chocolate Crunch Cookies

Easy to make, with outstanding results. Crispy outside, chewy inside—so good!

Large eggs	2	2
Cooking oil	1/4 cup	60 mL
Box of devil's food cake mix (2 layer size)	1	1
Skor (or Heath) bars (1 1/2 oz., 39 g, each), coarsely chopped	3	3

Beat eggs and cooking oil in medium bowl until combined. Add cake mix. Mix well.

(continued on next page)

Add Skor pieces. Stir until combined. Roll into balls, using 2 tsp. (10 mL) for each cookie. Arrange 2 inches (5 cm) apart on greased cookie sheets. Bake in 350°F (175°C) oven for about 10 minutes until tops are domed and cracked. Let stand on cookie sheets for 2 minutes before removing to wire racks to cool. Makes about 4 dozen (48) cookies.

1 cookie: 69 Calories; 2.2 g Total Fat (0.9 g Mono, 0.4 g Poly, 0.7 g Sat); 10 mg Cholesterol; 2 g Carbohydrate; trace Fibre; trace Protein; 17 mg Sodium

Pictured on page 125.

Quick Cheesecake Pie

A tangy, light-textured filling in a sweet graham crust.
Delectable cheesecake flavour, without the fuss!

Tub of strawberry light spreadable cream cheese, softened	8 oz.	250 g
Icing (confectioner's) sugar	1 cup	250 mL
Frozen whipped topping, thawed, divided	2 cups	500 mL
Graham cracker crust (9 inch, 22 cm, diameter)	1	1

Beat cream cheese and icing sugar in large bowl until smooth.

Reserve 1/2 cup (125 mL) whipped topping in small bowl. Fold remaining whipped topping into cream cheese mixture. Spread in graham crust. Chill for at least 1 hour until firm. Cut into 6 wedges. Serve with a dollop of reserved whipped topping. Serves 6.

1 serving: 457 Calories; 24.7 g Total Fat (7.5 g Mono, 3.2 g Poly, 12.5 g Sat); 26 mg Cholesterol; 55 g Carbohydrate; 0 g Fibre; 6 g Protein; 525 mg Sodium

Paré Pointer

Lawyers are disbarred, clergy defrocked, electricians delighted, musicians denoted, cowboys deranged, and dry cleaners depressed.

Cranberry Macaroons

You'll be over the moon when you taste these easy-to-make macaroons! Extra special with tart cranberries.

Egg whites (large), room temperature	2	2
Granulated sugar	3/4 cup	175 mL
Shredded (long thread) coconut	3/4 cup	175 mL
Chopped dried cranberries	3/4 cup	175 mL

Beat egg whites and a pinch of salt in medium bowl until soft peaks form. Add sugar 1 tbsp. (15 mL) at a time, beating constantly until stiff peaks form and sugar is dissolved.

Fold in coconut and cranberries. Drop, using 1 tbsp. (15 mL) for each cookie, about 2 inches (5 cm) apart onto greased cookie sheets. Bake in 325°F (160°C) oven for about 15 minutes until golden. Let stand on cookie sheets for 5 minutes before removing to wire racks to cool. Makes about 32 macaroons.

1 macaroon: 40 Calories; 1.5 g Total Fat (0.1 g Mono, 0 g Poly, 1.3 g Sat); 0 mg Cholesterol; 7 g Carbohydrate; 1 g Fibre; 0 g Protein; 4 mg Sodium

Pumpkin Streusel Squares

This delightful cake is moist and cratered in the middle. Serve with a scoop of ice cream or a dollop of whipped cream.

Box of orange cake mix (2 layer size), divided	1	1
Hard margarine (or butter), melted	3/4 cup	175 mL
Large eggs, divided	3	3
Can of pumpkin pie filling	19 oz.	540 mL

Reserve 3/4 cup (175 mL) cake mix in small bowl. Beat remaining cake mix, margarine, 1 egg and 1/4 cup (60 mL) water in medium bowl for about 1 minute until smooth. Spread in greased 9 × 13 inch (22 × 33 cm) pan.

(continued on next page)

Desserts & Snacks

Beat remaining 2 eggs in same bowl until frothy. Add pie filling. Beat well. Pour over batter in pan. Sift reserved cake mix over top. Bake in 350°F (175°C) oven for about 45 minutes until set and wooden pick inserted in centre comes out moist but not wet with batter. Do not overbake. Cool. Cuts into 24 squares.

1 square: 182 Calories; 9.2 g Total Fat (5.2 g Mono, 1.6 g Poly, 1.8 g Sat); 27 mg Cholesterol; 24 g Carbohydrate; 0 g Fibre; 2 g Protein; 272 mg Sodium

Express Tropical Trifle

A taste of the tropics—pineapple sweetens the ever-popular banana cream combo and moistens a layer of fluffy vanilla cake.

Package of Twinkies, each halved lengthwise	11 oz.	300 g
Cans of crushed pineapple (14 oz., 398 mL, each), with juice	2	2
Large bananas, sliced	4	4
Frozen whipped topping, thawed	4 cups	1 L

Arrange Twinkie halves, filling-side up, in ungreased 9 x 13 inch (22 x 33 cm) baking dish.

Spoon 1 can of pineapple with juice onto cakes. Scatter banana slices over pineapple. Spoon remaining can of pineapple with juice on top of banana.

Spread whipped topping over pineapple to sides of baking dish. Chill for 2 hours. Serves 12.

1 serving: 252 Calories; 9.8 g Total Fat (1.6 g Mono, 1.1 g Poly, 6.5 g Sat); 4 mg Cholesterol; 42 g Carbohydrate; 1 g Fibre; 2 g Protein; 99 mg Sodium

Paré Pointer

What do you have if you cross a centipede with a parrot?
A walkie–talkie!

Liquid Gold Sauce

*This warm sauce will add sparkle to vanilla ice cream or a
chocolate dessert. Tastes great over angel food cake and berries too!*

Granulated sugar	1 cup	250 mL
Milk	1/2 cup	125 mL
Butter (or hard margarine)	1/4 cup	60 mL
Orange liqueur	2 tbsp.	30 mL

Heat and stir first 3 ingredients in medium saucepan on medium until
boiling and sugar is dissolved. Boil gently for 5 minutes. Remove from heat.

Add liqueur. Stir. Makes about 1 cup (250 mL).

*2 tbsp. (30 mL): 165 Calories; 6.1 g Total Fat (1.8 g Mono, 0.2 g Poly, 3.8 g Sat); 17 mg Cholesterol;
26 g Carbohydrate; 0 g Fibre; 1 g Protein; 68 mg Sodium*

Lively Lime Pie

*A quick and easy tropical treat! Perfect for a
summer luncheon. Keep in the freezer until ready to serve.*

Block of cream cheese, softened	8 oz.	250 g
Can of sweetened condensed milk	11 oz.	300 mL
Medium limes	2	2
Graham cracker crust (9 inch, 22 cm, diameter)	1	1

Beat cream cheese in medium bowl for about 3 minutes until smooth.
Slowly add condensed milk, beating constantly until combined.

Grate 2 tsp. (10 mL) lime zest into small bowl. Squeeze lime juice. Add
water, if needed, to make 1/2 cup (125 mL). Add to cream cheese mixture.
Beat well. Spread in graham crust. Freeze for at least 4 hours until firm.
Cuts into 8 wedges.

*1 wedge: 417 Calories; 22.6 g Total Fat (7.7 g Mono, 2.6 g Poly, 11.1 g Sat); 51 mg Cholesterol;
48 g Carbohydrate; trace Fibre; 8 g Protein; 325 mg Sodium*

Brownie Cookies

Dense and delicious two-bite treats. Keep lots on hand—they won't last long!

Unsweetened chocolate baking squares (1 oz., 28 g, each), chopped	2	2
Chocolate hazelnut spread	1/4 cup	60 mL
Graham cracker crumbs	2 cups	500 mL
Can of sweetened condensed milk	11 oz.	300 mL

Melt chocolate in large heavy saucepan on lowest heat, stirring often, until almost melted. Do not overheat. Remove from heat. Add chocolate hazelnut spread. Stir until smooth.

Add graham crumbs and condensed milk. Stir until stiff batter forms. Drop, using 1 tbsp. (15 mL) for each cookie, about 2 inches (5 cm) apart onto greased cookie sheets. Bake in 375°F (190°C) oven for 8 to 10 minutes until edges are set. Centres will be soft. Immediately remove to wire racks to cool. Makes about 3 dozen (36) cookies.

1 cookie: 75 Calories; 3.3 g Total Fat (1.3 g Mono, 0.4 g Poly, 1.4 g Sat); 4 mg Cholesterol; 10 g Carbohydrate; trace Fibre; 2 g Protein; 53 mg Sodium

Peanut Butter Fudge

Fluffy fudge quickly made from simple ingredients. Sure to disappear just as fast! Serve chilled.

Granulated sugar	2 cups	500 mL
Milk	1/2 cup	125 mL
Chunky peanut butter	1 1/2 cups	375 mL
Jar of marshmallow creme	7 oz.	198 g

Heat and stir sugar and milk in heavy medium saucepan on medium until boiling and sugar is dissolved. Boil gently for about 3 minutes, stirring constantly, until slightly thickened. Remove from heat.

Add peanut butter and marshmallow creme. Stir until smooth. Spread in greased 8 × 8 inch (20 × 20 cm) pan. Chill for at least 3 hours until set. Cuts into 64 squares.

1 square: 74 Calories; 3.2 g Total Fat (1.5 g Mono, 0.9 g Poly, 0.6 g Sat); 0 mg Cholesterol; 11 g Carbohydrate; trace Fibre; 2 g Protein; 34 mg Sodium

Cranapple Tarts

A fresh, tart filling that's a lovely ruby red. Dress these
up with a whipped cream rosette or a dusting of icing sugar.

Small cooking apples (such as McIntosh), peeled and cut up	2	2
Fresh (or frozen, thawed) cranberries	2 cups	500 mL
White corn syrup	1 cup	250 mL
Unbaked tart shells	24	24

Process first 3 ingredients in blender or food processor until cranberries are finely chopped. Transfer to medium bowl.

Place tart shells on baking sheets. Spoon fruit mixture into shells. Bake in 400°F (205°C) oven for about 20 minutes until pastry is golden and filling is bubbling. Remove to wire racks to cool. Makes 24 tarts.

1 tart: 115 Calories; 4.1 g Total Fat (2 g Mono, 0.5 g Poly, 1.3 g Sat); 0 mg Cholesterol;
20 g Carbohydrate; 1 g Fibre; 1 g Protein; 98 mg Sodium

Butterscotch Pumpkin Pie

This custard-style dessert is a delicious alternative to traditional
pumpkin pie. You can freeze the second pie to enjoy later.

Large eggs	3	3
Butterscotch ripple ice cream, melted	3 cups	750 mL
Can of pumpkin pie filling	19 oz.	540 mL
Graham cracker crusts (9 inch, 22 cm, diameter, each)	2	2

Beat eggs in large bowl until frothy. Add ice cream and pie filling. Stir until smooth.

Pour filling into graham crusts. Bake in 350°F (175°C) oven for about 45 to 50 minutes until filling is set. Let stand on wire racks until cooled completely. Each pie cuts into 8 wedges, for a total of 16 wedges.

1 wedge: 254 Calories; 11.3 g Total Fat (4.6 g Mono, 2.3 g Poly, 3.6 g Sat); 52 mg Cholesterol;
36 g Carbohydrate; 0 g Fibre; 4 g Protein; 284 mg Sodium

Desserts & Snacks

Butterscotch Shortbread

Short on time? Here's a speedy answer to what to serve for tea!
The brown sugar creates the butterscotch flavour in this rich shortbread.

Butter, softened	1 cup	250 mL
Brown sugar, packed	2/3 cup	150 mL
All-purpose flour	2 cups	500 mL
Graham cracker crumbs	1/2 cup	125 mL

Cream butter and brown sugar in medium bowl.

Combine flour and graham crumbs in small bowl. Add to butter mixture. Mix until soft, slightly crumbly dough forms. Turn out onto lightly floured surface. Knead for about 2 minutes until smooth. Press into ungreased 8 × 8 inch (20 × 20 cm) pan. Prick top of dough in several places with a fork. Score dough into 12 rectangles with sharp knife. Score rectangles diagonally into 24 triangles. Bake in 300°F (150°C) oven for about 30 minutes until edges are golden. Let stand in pan on wire rack until cooled completely. Cut along scoring into 24 triangles.

1 triangle: 144 Calories; 8.4 g Total Fat (2.4 g Mono, 0.4 g Poly, 5.1 g Sat); 22 mg Cholesterol; 16 g Carbohydrate; trace Fibre; 1 g Protein; 97 mg Sodium

Baked Pears

A simple, elegant dessert. Nice as is, or serve with vanilla ice cream.

Fresh pears, peeled, halved lengthwise, cores removed	4	4
Corn syrup	1/2 cup	125 mL
Lemon juice	2 tbsp.	30 mL
Ground cinnamon	1/2 tsp.	2 mL

Arrange pear halves, cut-side down, in ungreased 3 quart (3 L) casserole. Score decorative pattern on pears.

Combine remaining 3 ingredients in small cup. Pour over pears. Bake, covered, in 350°F (175°C) oven for about 30 minutes until tender. Spoon sauce from casserole over individual servings. Serves 4.

1 serving: 170 Calories; 0.1 g Total Fat (0 g Mono, 0 g Poly, 0 g Sat); 0 mg Cholesterol; 46 g Carbohydrate; 3 g Fibre; 0 g Protein; 56 mg Sodium

Mudsicle Pie

Serve this pie straight from the freezer.

Box of instant chocolate pudding powder (6 serving size)	1	1
Chocolate ice cream, softened	2 cups	500 mL
Chocolate milk	1/2 cup	125 mL
Chocolate crumb crust (9 inch, 22 cm, diameter)	1	1

Beat first 3 ingredients in medium bowl for about 2 minutes until thickened.

Spread filling in crumb crust. Freeze for at least 3 hours until firm. Cuts into 8 wedges.

1 wedge: 304 Calories; 13.2 g Total Fat (5.5 g Mono, 2.4 g Poly, 4.6 g Sat); 13 mg Cholesterol; 45 g Carbohydrate; trace Fibre; 4 g Protein; 527 mg Sodium

Orange Cream Cake

Dust with icing sugar for a pretty finish.

Large oranges	2 – 3	2 – 3
Box of orange cake mix (2 layer size)	1	1
Large eggs	4	4
Envelope of dessert topping (not prepared)	1	1

Grate 2 tbsp. (30 mL) orange zest into large bowl. Squeeze and add 1 cup (250 mL) orange juice.

Add remaining 3 ingredients. Beat on medium for about 2 minutes until smooth. Pour into greased and floured 12 cup (3 L) bundt pan. Bake in 350°F (175°C) oven for about 45 minutes until wooden pick inserted in centre of cake comes out clean. Let stand in pan on wire rack for 15 minutes. Tap pan gently on countertop to loosen cake. Invert onto wire rack to cool completely. Cuts into 12 wedges.

1 wedge: 245 Calories; 8.2 g Total Fat (2.8 g Mono, 2.2 g Poly, 2.6 g Sat); 73 mg Cholesterol; 39 g Carbohydrate; trace Fibre; 4 g Protein; 312 mg Sodium

Anise Orange Ice

Heady licorice-scented orange sherbet. Incredibly refreshing!

Granulated sugar	2 1/2 cups	625 mL
Star anise	3	3
Frozen concentrated orange juice	1/2 cup	125 mL
Grated orange zest	1 tsp.	5 mL

Combine sugar, anise and 5 cups (1.25 L) water in medium saucepan. Bring to a boil. Reduce heat to medium. Boil gently for 5 minutes. Remove from heat.

Add concentrated orange juice and zest. Stir. Discard anise. Cool. Chill, covered, for at least 3 hours until very cold. Pour into ice cream maker (see Note). Follow manufacturer's instructions. Makes about 6 cups (1.5 L).

1 cup (250 mL): 381 Calories; 0.1 g Total Fat (0 g Mono, 0 g Poly, 0 g Sat); 0 mg Cholesterol; 98 g Carbohydrate; trace Fibre; 1 g Protein; 2 mg Sodium

Note: If you don't have an ice cream maker, pour the mixture into a 9 x 9 inch (22 x 22 cm) pan. Freeze, stirring every hour for 4 hours. The texture will be flakier, but the flavour will not be affected.

Ginger Cream Fudge

Zippy ginger and a snappy crunch in a smooth white fudge. Makes a great gift!

Can of sweetened condensed milk	11 oz.	300 mL
White chocolate chips	2 1/2 cups	625 mL
Gingersnaps, broken into small pieces	10	10
Minced crystallized ginger	2 tbsp.	30 mL

Heat condensed milk in heavy medium saucepan on medium-low for about 7 minutes, stirring occasionally, until hot but not boiling. Add chocolate chips. Stir until smooth. Remove from heat.

Add gingersnap pieces and ginger. Stir. Spread in greased 8 x 8 inch (20 x 20 cm) pan. Chill for at least 2 hours until firm. Cuts into 64 squares.

1 square: 69 Calories; 2.9 g Total Fat (1 g Mono, 0.1 g Poly, 1.6 g Sat); 4 mg Cholesterol; 10 g Carbohydrate; trace Fibre; 1 g Protein; 32 mg Sodium

Fruity Nut Clusters

A combination of sweet and crunchy in a blond haystack treat.
Keeps well in an airtight container for one week.

White chocolate chips	2 cups	500 mL
Dry chow mein noodles	2/3 cup	150 mL
Salted peanuts	1/2 cup	125 mL
Chopped dried apricot	1/3 cup	75 mL

Heat chocolate chips in heavy medium saucepan on lowest heat, stirring often, until almost melted. Do not overheat. Remove from heat. Stir until smooth.

Add remaining 3 ingredients. Stir until coated. Drop, using 1 tbsp. (15 mL) for each cluster, onto waxed paper-lined baking sheet. Let stand until set. Makes about 22 clusters.

1 cluster: 120 Calories; 7.2 g Total Fat (2.5 g Mono, 0.9 g Poly, 3.2 g Sat); 4 mg Cholesterol; 13 g Carbohydrate; 1 g Fibre; 2 g Protein; 50 mg Sodium

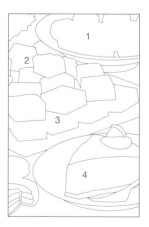

1. VIP Cookies, page 128
2. Blondie Brownies, page 129
3. Snap Brownies, page 132
4. Strawberry Margarita Pie, page 130

Props courtesy of: Casa Bugatti
                            Cherison Enterprises Inc.

Desserts & Snacks

Marble Top Snack Cake

A marbled top adds a dramatic flair to these squares. Great with coffee or tea.

Large eggs, divided	5	5
Package of brownie mix	2 lbs.	900 g
Block of cream cheese, softened	8 oz.	250 g
Brown sugar, packed	1/2 cup	125 mL

Beat 3 eggs in large bowl until frothy. Add brownie mix and 1/2 cup (125 mL) water. Beat until smooth. Spread in greased 9 × 13 inch (22 × 33 cm) pan.

Beat cream cheese, brown sugar and remaining 2 eggs in medium bowl until smooth. Pour over brownie mixture. Swirl knife through batter to create marbled effect. Bake in 350°F (175°C) oven for about 50 minutes until wooden pick inserted in centre comes out moist but not wet with batter. Do not overbake. Cool. Cuts into 24 squares.

1 square: 233 Calories; 10.3 g Total Fat (3.3 g Mono, 2.3 g Poly, 3.9 g Sat); 56 mg Cholesterol; 34 g Carbohydrate; 0 g Fibre; 4 g Protein; 159 mg Sodium

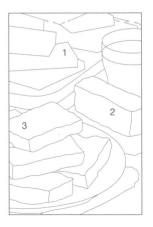

1. Hit-The-Trail Bars, page 131
2. Breakfast Bars, page 52
3. Grab-And-Go Squares, page 130

Props courtesy of: Out of the Fire Studio

Crunchy Cherry Cobbler

Cherry and pineapple are tucked under a sweet, crunchy crust that delivers a big vanilla taste. Double the cherries if you want a deeper fruit layer. Serve warm or cold with vanilla ice cream.

Can of cherry pie filling	19 oz.	540 mL
Can of crushed pineapple (with juice)	14 oz.	398 mL
Hard margarine (or butter)	1/2 cup	125 mL
Box of yellow (or white) cake mix (2 layer size)	1	1

Spread cherry pie filling in ungreased 9 × 13 inch (22 × 33 cm) baking dish. Spoon pineapple with juice on top of cherries.

Melt margarine in large saucepan on medium. Remove from heat. Add cake mix. Stir until moistened. Scatter over pineapple in baking dish. Bake in 350°F (175°C) oven for about 50 minutes until golden. Serves 15.

1 serving: 271 Calories; 10.6 g Total Fat (5.9 g Mono, 2.2 g Poly, 2 g Sat); 1 mg Cholesterol; 43 g Carbohydrate; trace Fibre; 2 g Protein; 309 mg Sodium

Fiesta Popcorn

Make this southwestern-style popcorn to share with all your amigos.

Grated Parmesan cheese	1/2 cup	125 mL
Chili powder	1 tbsp.	15 mL
Lemon pepper	1 tsp.	5 mL
Bag of butter-flavoured microwave popcorn	3 1/2 oz.	99 g

Combine first 3 ingredients in small bowl.

Prepare popcorn according to package directions. Put into large bowl. Sprinkle with Parmesan cheese mixture. Toss until coated. Makes about 8 cups (2 L).

1 cup (250 mL): 61 Calories; 3.7 g Total Fat (1 g Mono, 0.8 g Poly, 1.5 g Sat); 5 mg Cholesterol; 4 g Carbohydrate; 1 g Fibre; 3 g Protein; 256 mg Sodium

Desserts & Snacks

Berry Mini-Cheesecakes

Berry jam swirled in creamy cheesecakes. A yummy dessert
that freezes well. Keep these on hand for unexpected company.

Cream-filled chocolate cookies	12	12
Tubs of berry spreadable cream cheese (8 oz., 250 g, each)	2	2
Large eggs	2	2
Berry jam	2 tbsp.	30 mL

Line 12 ungreased muffin cups with paper liners. Spray liners with cooking spray. Place cookies in liners.

Beat cream cheese until smooth. Add eggs 1 at a time, beating well after each addition. Spoon onto cookies.

Measure jam into small cup. Stir until smooth. Spoon onto cream cheese mixture. Swirl with wooden pick to create marbled effect. Bake in 325°F (160°C) oven for about 20 minutes until set. Let stand in pan on wire rack for 1 hour. Chill for at least 1 hour until firm. Makes 12 mini-cheesecakes.

1 mini-cheesecake: 161 Calories; 11 g Total Fat (4 g Mono, 0.7 g Poly, 5.3 g Sat); 62 mg Cholesterol; 11 g Carbohydrate; trace Fibre; 5 g Protein; 363 mg Sodium

Pictured on page 71.

Paré Pointer

An accountant solves a problem that you didn't know you had,
and explains it in a way that you don't understand.

Berry Shortcake

Strawberry shortcake is even more inviting
with the added goodness of blueberries. Yum!

Vanilla sponge cake, 2 layers (6 inch, 15 cm, diameter)	1	1
Container of frozen strawberries in light syrup, thawed	15 oz.	425 g
Frozen blueberries, thawed	1 1/2 cups	375 mL
Frozen whipped topping, thawed (or whipped cream)	1 cup	250 mL

Place 1 cake layer, flat-side up, on large serving plate. Poke cake in several places with wooden skewer.

Spoon 1/2 of strawberries with syrup onto cake, allowing some syrup to run down side. Sprinkle with 1/2 of blueberries. Cover with second cake layer, flat-side down. Poke second cake layer in several places with wooden skewer. Top with remaining berries and syrup. Chill, covered, for at least 2 hours to allow cake to absorb syrup.

Cut into 6 wedges. Serve with a dollop of whipped topping. Serves 6.

1 serving: 239 Calories; 4.8 g Total Fat (0.6 g Mono, 0.3 g Poly, 3.2 g Sat); 43 mg Cholesterol; 49 g Carbohydrate; 3 g Fibre; 3 g Protein; 106 mg Sodium

Paré Pointer
You know you're in trouble when your
knees buckle but your belt won't.

Measurement Tables

Throughout this book measurements are given in Conventional and Metric measure. To compensate for differences between the two measurements due to rounding, a full metric measure is not always used. The cup used is the standard 8 fluid ounce. Temperature is given in degrees Fahrenheit and Celsius. Baking pan measurements are in inches and centimetres as well as quarts and litres. An exact metric conversion is given below as well as the working equivalent (Metric Standard Measure).

Spoons

Conventional Measure	Metric Exact Conversion Millilitre (mL)	Metric Standard Measure Millilitre (mL)
1/8 teaspoon (tsp.)	0.6 mL	0.5 mL
1/4 teaspoon (tsp.)	1.2 mL	1 mL
1/2 teaspoon (tsp.)	2.4 mL	2 mL
1 teaspoon (tsp.)	4.7 mL	5 mL
2 teaspoons (tsp.)	9.4 mL	10 mL
1 tablespoon (tbsp.)	14.2 mL	15 mL

Cups

Conventional Measure	Metric Exact Conversion Millilitre (mL)	Metric Standard Measure Millilitre (mL)
1/4 cup (4 tbsp.)	56.8 mL	60 mL
1/3 cup (5 1/3 tbsp.)	75.6 mL	75 mL
1/2 cup (8 tbsp.)	113.7 mL	125 mL
2/3 cup (10 2/3 tbsp.)	151.2 mL	150 mL
3/4 cup (12 tbsp.)	170.5 mL	175 mL
1 cup (16 tbsp.)	227.3 mL	250 mL
4 1/2 cups	1022.9 mL	1000 mL (1 L)

Dry Measurements

Conventional Measure Ounces (oz.)	Metric Exact Conversion Grams (g)	Metric Standard Measure Grams (g)
1 oz.	28.3 g	28 g
2 oz.	56.7 g	57 g
3 oz.	85.0 g	85 g
4 oz.	113.4 g	125 g
5 oz.	141.7 g	140 g
6 oz.	170.1 g	170 g
7 oz.	198.4 g	200 g
8 oz.	226.8 g	250 g
16 oz.	453.6 g	500 g
32 oz.	907.2 g	1000 g (1 kg)

Oven Temperatures

Fahrenheit (°F)	Celsius (°C)
175°	80°
200°	95°
225°	110°
250°	120°
275°	140°
300°	150°
325°	160°
350°	175°
375°	190°
400°	205°
425°	220°
450°	230°
475°	240°
500°	260°

Pans

Conventional Inches	Metric Centimetres
8x8 inch	20x20 cm
9x9 inch	22x22 cm
9x13 inch	22x33 cm
10x15 inch	25x38 cm
11x17 inch	28x43 cm
8x2 inch round	20x5 cm
9x2 inch round	22x5 cm
10x4 1/2 inch tube	25x11 cm
8x4x3 inch loaf	20x10x7.5 cm
9x5x3 inch loaf	22x12.5x7.5 cm

Casseroles

CANADA & BRITAIN		UNITED STATES	
Standard Size Casserole	Exact Metric Measure	Standard Size Casserole	Exact Metric Measure
1 qt. (5 cups)	1.13 L	1 qt. (4 cups)	900 mL
1 1/2 qts. (7 1/2 cups)	1.69 L	1 1/2 qts. (6 cups)	1.35 L
2 qts. (10 cups)	2.25 L	2 qts. (8 cups)	1.8 L
2 1/2 qts. (12 1/2 cups)	2.81 L	2 1/2 qts. (10 cups)	2.25 L
3 qts. (15 cups)	3.38 L	3 qts. (12 cups)	2.7 L
4 qts. (20 cups)	4.5 L	4 qts. (16 cups)	3.6 L
5 qts. (25 cups)	5.63 L	5 qts. (20 cups)	4.5 L

Recipe Index

152

H

I

L

M

N

O

155

Swiss Ham Bake

Anytime Casseroles, Page 106

Water	8 cups	2 L
Salt	1 tsp.	5 mL
Penne pasta	2 cups	500 mL
Milk	2 cups	500 mL
Diced cooked ham	1 1/2 cups	375 mL
Frozen cut green beans	0 pt	375 mL
Can of condensed cream of chicken soup	10 oz.	284 mL
Dijon mustard	1 tsp.	5 mL
Pepper	1/4 tsp.	1 mL
Fine dry bread crumbs	1/2 cup	125 mL
Grated Swiss cheese	1/4 cup	60 mL
Butter (or hard margarine), melted	2 tbsp.	30 mL

Combine water and salt in large saucepan. Bring to a boil. Add pasta. Boil, uncovered, for 14 to 16 minutes, stirring occasionally, until tender but firm. Drain. Return to same pot.

Add next 6 ingredients. Stir. Transfer to greased 9 x 13 inch (23 x 33 cm) baking dish.

Combine remaining 3 ingredients in small bowl. Sprinkle over top. Bake in 375°F (190°C) oven for about 30 minutes until bubbling and golden. Serves 6.

1 serving: 367 Calories; 16.0 g Total Fat (5.0 g Mono, 1.5 g Poly, 7.0 g Sat); 44 mg Cholesterol; 37 g Carbohydrate; 2 g Fibre; 18 g Protein; 868 mg Sodium

If you like what we've done with **cooking,** you'll **love** what we do with **crafts**!

Complete your Original Series Collection!

- ❏ 150 Delicious Squares
- ❏ Appetizers
- ❏ Cookies
- ❏ Barbecues
- ❏ Preserves
- ❏ Slow Cooker Recipes
- ❏ Stir-Fry
- ❏ Stews, Chilies & Chowders
- ❏ Fondues
- ❏ The Rookie Cook
- ❏ Sweet Cravings
- ❏ Year-Round Grilling
- ❏ Garden Greens
- ❏ Chinese Cooking
- ❏ The Beverage Book
- ❏ Slow Cooker Dinners
- ❏ 30-Minute Weekday Meals
- ❏ Potluck Dishes
- ❏ Ground Beef Recipes
- ❏ 4-Ingredient Recipes
- ❏ Kids' Healthy Cooking
- ❏ Mostly Muffins
- ❏ Soups
- ❏ Simple Suppers
- ❏ Diabetic Cooking
- ❏ Chicken Now
- ❏ Kids Do Snacks
- ❏ Low-Fat Express
- ❏ Choosing Sides
- ❏ Perfect Pasta & Sauces
- ❏ 30-Minute Diabetic Cooking
- ❏ Healthy In A Hurry
- ❏ Table For Two
- ❏ Catch Of The Day
- ❏ Kids Do Baking
- ❏ 5-Ingredient Slow Cooker Recipes
- ❏ Diabetic Dinners
- ❏ Easy Healthy Recipes
- ❏ 30-Minute Pantry
- ❏ Everyday Barbecuing
- ❏ Meal Salads
- ❏ Healthy Slow Cooker
- ❏ Breads
- ❏ Anytime Casseroles
  NEW February 1/11

Each Focus Series book is a mini feature event—priced to make collecting them all especially easy.

Focus Series

- ❏ Apple Appeal
- ❏ Berries & Cream
- ❏ Carrot Craze
- ❏ Chicken Breast Finesse
- ❏ Chilled Thrills
- ❏ Chocolate Squared
- ❏ Coffee Cake Classics
- ❏ Cookie Jar Classics
- ❏ Cranberrys Cravings
- ❏ Dip, Dunk & Dab
- ❏ Easy Roasting
- ❏ Fab Finger Food
- ❏ Fruit Squared
- ❏ Hearty Soups
- ❏ Hot Bites
- ❏ Lemon Lime Zingers
- ❏ Mushroom Magic
- ❏ Salads To Go
- ❏ Shrimp Delicious
- ❏ Simmering Stews
- ❏ Simply Vegetarian
- ❏ Sips
- ❏ Skewered
- ❏ So Strawberry
- ❏ Splendid Spuds
- ❏ Steak Sizzle
- ❏ Sweet Dreams
- ❏ That's A Wrap
- ❏ Tomato Temptations
- ❏ Tossed
- ❏ Warm Desserts
- ❏ Zucchini Zone